CW00704147

CHINESE PAINTING

CHINESE PAINTING

FRANCISCA TING

B T BATSFORD LIMITED
LONDON

For my Father and Mother

First published 1990

© Francisca Ting 1990

ISBN 0 7134 5841 0

Typeset by Servis Filmsetting Ltd,
Manchester
and printed in Hong Kong

For the publishers
B T Batsford Limited
4 Fitzhardinge Street
London W1H 0AH

CONTENTS

FOREWORD

Today more people than ever before are interested in Chinese painting. Beginners naturally have many obstacles to overcome before they can achieve technical success, but the age-old techniques are extremely economical, using predominantly black Chinese ink, simple brushstrokes and dots. For this minimalist approach, outlines are frequently suggested rather than actually drawn. The artistically placed strokes and shadings, together with the clever use of space, combine to produce the delicate effects which characterize this art form.

Chinese painting is not as difficult as is often imagined. The key is to know the techniques and then to master them by conscientious practice. This is the starting point for personal expression in art. Practice and experience will lead to greater brush control; brush control is essential in order to achieve the subtle tones and effects which convey the images and ideas so beautifully and uniquely Chinese.

In writing this book, I have tried to visualize all the possible difficulties that may beset the beginner and the ways in which they may be overcome. I certainly hope many of you will become interested at least, in trying your hand at Chinese painting.

A hundred butterflies

INTRODUCTION

This book is an attempt to guide you, as an interested amateur, step by step towards the mastering of the basic techniques in Chinese painting. I would like to emphasize that this is not just for those with some experience, but for beginners too, and I have tried to show novices how to appreciate Chinese painting and increase their pleasure and understanding of the art, for it is something which really repays study. Many people believe that those with inherent ability can become great artists, whether taught or not. However, as far as Chinese painting is concerned, it

is reasonable to argue that little beauty may be created without some knowledge of technique and materials. Thus a few technical hints can hardly offend and may often save you many heart-breaking failures.

It is important for a beginner foreign to Chinese culture and tradition to understand the Chinese artist's approach to the subject and the mental background behind the art. Art in China has evolved from centuries-old beliefs and traditions. Underlying the apparent simplicity, harmony and the aura of serenity of a composition, there is a philos-

ophy that is as old as Chinese civilization. It is a philosophy that sees a unifying pattern in all natural life forms. Every individual life form is of kin and each has the power to communicate its own life-spirit, referred to as *ch'i*. Man is not conceived of as the lord of creation, but as one among innumerable orders of beings in the universe. This acceptance of man's true place in the vastness of the universe, and the artist's sympathy with every form of life outside humanity as well as within it, are the two most important factors underlying Chinese Art.

Chrysanthemum and bamboo

Hsieh Ho (sixth century) in his famous book *Ku-hua p'in-lu* formulated a set of six principles by which a painting should be judged. The most important is the first, *ch'i-yün sheng-tung*, frequently translated as 'rhythmic vitality'. Accordingly, the supreme virtue in a composition is its capacity to embody and communicate the universal spirit of life, *ch'i*. To transmit *ch'i*, *ku* is important. *Ku* refers to the structural strength of the brushstroke. It is *ku* which expresses the vital inner spirit of the life form painted. Thus, Hsieh Ho's second principle is *ku fa yung pi*, translated as 'brushwork to indicate bones and structure'.

The ultimate goal of a Chinese artist is to capture *ch'i* through brushwork, hence the flowing and rhythmical movement that one finds in every Chinese composition. Without *ch'i*, without a sense of vitality in handling the brush, a painting is lifeless. The brushstroke is the central fact of Chinese painting throughout its history: for the Chinese artist, the brush line is the primary descriptive and expressive means and the chief criterion of excellence in a painting.

The single brushstroke is the 'origin of all existence', wrote Tao-chi (seventeenth century). The artist uses the single brushstroke to draft objects carefully to give likeness, Hsieh Ho's third principle *ying wu hsiang hsing*, and to give tone and colour in order to fit the character of the object, Hsieh Ho's fourth principle *sui lei fu ts'ai*. Hsieh Ho's fifth principle, *ching ying wei chih*, refers to careful planning and design for a harmonious composition. Chinese artists do not paint what is before their eyes. Composition is the outcome of long observation. When they paint, they have the whole picture in their mind. They concentrate on their theme and the feeling it evokes. In this way they infuse the brush with feeling and spirit and as a result fill it with *ch'i*. This is the ultimate goal. The complete representation of an object or scene is not the aim – all irrelevant details are left out. Hence, the apparent simplicity.

This introduction is incom-

Drunk with the scent of summer

plete without a word on copying. Copying or imitating an ancient model has always been part of the training of the student artist. It is so important that Hsieh Ho put it down as the sixth principle, although it does not really belong to the same category as the first five. Li Lung Mien, the most renowned of all the Sung Masters, spent much time copying old masterpieces. Chang Dai Chien (1899–1983) said that one should start with copying the old masters. He himself spent much time and took great pains to copy Tao-chi, better known as Shih-t'ao (c.1641–1710). The emphasis on copying was so overwhelming that a whole generation of artists could hold up one particular artist as a model to be imitated,

as was, for example, Huang Kung-wang (one of the four great Yüan masters), by the seventeenth-century artists. Artists firmly believed that this was the best way to achieve success and they took great pride in acknowledging the artist whom they imitated on their works.

This practice is completely alien to the Western mind, but Chinese artists themselves cautioned that one should never copy just one artist. They recommended that a student artist should copy one model, and then move on to copy other styles. As a student artist, the more ideas you have to express, the greater the number of different techniques you will be forced to find. Once the technical possibilities

are known, a personal style should arise naturally. A perfect confidence in the technical means at your disposal will encourage you to express yourself to the fullest, and each composition will become a voyage of self-discovery.

Finally, to those who argue that one cannot be a skilled artist just by reading a book, I wish to add that I agree absolutely. However, there is no need to be a skilled artist. A few effective basic techniques learned from a book and practised until they become second nature will surely enable you to produce your own creative compositions, that are bound to give you much personal satisfaction and moments of joy.

A dragonfly in summer

1

CHINESE PAINTING

Mowtan peonies and Chansou niao. The 'King of flowers' symbolizes spring, and love and beauty; the birds represent longevity

A Short History of Chinese Painting

Chronological Table

Shang (c.1550–1030 BC)
Chou (c.1030–256 BC)
Western Chou
Eastern Chou
'Spring & Autumn' period
Warring States period

Confucius formed for China a code of ethics based on early Chinese rites and ceremonies. Lao-tzu gave to China the doctrine of Taoism, a kind of mystic philosophy of nature. Taoism grew into a full-fledged Church with a canon of scriptures, its own hierarchy and temples. It was later adopted as the official religion. The philosophies formulated by Confucius and Lao-tzu have governed Chinese thinking right up to the present day, and they have a profound influence on the development of Chinese painting.

Ch'in (221–207 BC)

Towards the end of the Chou period, the Empire began to split up into various small states, and fierce feuds developed. Three dynasties, the Ch'u, Ch'i and Ch'in, fought for political control during the Warring States period, and in 221 BC the Ch'in dynasty gained power.

Han (202 BC–AD 220)
Western Han
Hsin
Eastern Han

The Han, after a great struggle with the Ch'in, succeeded to power. The Han Dynasty is con-sidered one of the greatest in Chinese history. Its most significant achievement was the creation of a common economic and social system, a uniform ideology and a set of customs.

Three Kingdoms (221–265)
Shu (Han)
Wei
Wu

The fall of the Han Dynasty caused the Empire to disintegrate. A period of wars, unrest and changes ensued. Barbarian invaders conquered the whole of northern China. The Empire split into two parts.

Northern Dynasties (265–581)
Northern Wei
Eastern Wei
Western Wei
Northern Ch'i
Northern Chou

The customs of Tartar invaders who conquered and ruled the whole of northern China became assimilated into the Chinese culture and tradition. Chinese civilization was not set aside. The Wei rulers fostered Buddhism, an alien religion brought in from India.

Southern Dynasties (265–581)
Chin
Eastern Chin
Liu Sung
Southern Ch'i
Liang
Ch'en

The period of 'Southern Dynasties' (or 'Six Dynasties') refers to southern China, which was still governed by China's own native rulers. It is in the south that painting took firm root during this period.

Sui (581–618)

China was unified under the Sui Dynasty but there were no strong leaders to rule the vast Empire.

T'ang (618–906)

The T'ang Dynasty revived the glory of the Han Empire and re-established its continental hegemony. Education, art, culture, and international trade flourished. Repeated peasant uprisings weakened the empire during the ninth century.

Five Dynasties (907–960)
Later Liang
Later T'ang
Later Chin
Later Han
Later Chou

With the last T'ang Emperor dethroned in 907, China was again split into small states ruled by short-lived Emperors. China fell into disorder.

Sung (960–1279)
Northern Sung
Southern Sung

The Sung Emperors failed to revive the splendour and greatness of the T'ang Dynasty. They suffered one defeat after another from tribes coming from the north and west. 'Northern Sung' refers to the period 960–1126, when China was ruled by the Sung Emperors from their capital K'ai-fen in Honan, northern China. In 1127, the Jurcher Tartars seized and ruled northern China. From 1127 to 1279, the Sung rulers ruled southern China from their new capital Hangchow in Chekiang Province. This period is known as Southern Sung.

Finally, the Sung Emperors fell under Genghis Khan.

Yüan (Mongols) (1260–1368)

This century of Mongolian rule was a humiliating period in Chinese history. However, while the Yüan Dynasty changed laws and institutions, the culture of the Chinese people continued to develop along traditional lines.

Ming (1368–1644)

Chu Yüan-chang, a simple peasant, headed a rebellious army, rid China of her Mongol rulers and founded the Ming Dynasty. By the fifteenth century, China was the richest and most powerful empire in the world.

Ch'ing (Manchus) (1644–1912)

A similar peasant uprising to the one which brought the Ming rulers to power also caused its downfall. The Nuchen tribes of Manchuria occupied Peking after the fall of the Ming. Agriculture, industry and commerce progressed. China gradually opened her doors to the West. First came the Portuguese, followed by the Spaniards, the Dutch and finally the British. The Opium War opened the door to the foreign exploitation of China. The nineteenth-century wars with the Western powers were disastrous for the Chinese economy, for the traditional organization of Chinese society and for imperial China herself.

Republic of China (1912–1948)

China became a Republic in 1912, with Sun Yat-sen as her first President. Decades of fighting

and civil wars followed, which ended in the proclamation of the People's Republic of China in 1949, under the leadership of Chairman Mao Tse-tung.

People's Republic of China (1949–)

The modernization of China under Communist rule.

PAINTING IN THE PRE-SUNG DYNASTIES

The earliest surviving examples of true painting in China are on two fragments of silk dating from around the third century BC of the later Chou Period. These silk fragments, together with a bamboo brush with a rabbit's fur tip, and other writing and painting materials, were excavated from tombs at Chang-sha in the present-day Hunan Province. The pictures, symbolic representations of humans, demons, animals and plants, were drawn in fine, black-ink brushline with washes of colour. These pictures are proof that as early as the third century BC Chinese painting had already acquired a basic and orthodox technique and mode of representation. Beautiful pictures adorn lacquer bowls, dishes, boxes, trays and bronze vessels, found in tombs of the late Chou period, and are painted in black, red or white.

Historical records indicate that painting had made tremendous progress by the time of the Han Dynasty. We are told of wall-paintings in the imperial palaces showing mythological subjects and illustrious people, as well as illustrations of historical events or classical texts. Tombs of the Han period show lively compositions of human figures, intri-

cate scenes and landscapes engraved on stones, tiles and slabs of bricks. Portraits and frescoes have their beginnings during the Han period. The themes are most often Confucian. That Confucianism, with its emphasis on social duty and reverence for the past, had extended its influence to painting, can be seen in a painting by Ku K'ai-chih (c.344–406), the most famous artist of the fourth century. The painting, known as *The Admonitions of the Instructress in the Palace* now hangs in the British Museum. The scenes on the scroll depict an address to the ladies of the imperial household, counselling them, no doubt, on modesty, filial piety and other Confucian virtues.

Ku K'ai-chih also painted large frescoes of Buddhist subjects, since it was during this period that Buddhism was established. Indian statues and paintings were imported into China and these formed the models for Buddhist artists. The introduction of Buddhism gave a great impetus to works with religious motifs as can be seen in the frescoes in the caves of Tunhuang in West Kansu Province in north-west China. There are over 330 caves at Tunhuang, whose walls are all covered with religious paintings. The 'Caves of the thousand Buddhas', as they are known, also house numerous giant statues of Buddha. These frescoes and statues date back to the Northern Wei and Sui periods (fifth and sixth centuries) through to the T'ang, Five Dynasties and the Sung Dynasty (twelfth century).

Tunhuang has also yielded a whole series of Buddhist paintings on silk dating back to 864. However, they are mostly of the late T'ang period of the ninth and tenth centuries. The subjects of most of these paintings are the Buddhist conception of paradise, figures of *bodhisattvas*, or scenes from Buddha legend.

Along with Buddhism came the technique of illusionistic shading to give the appearance of solidity to a composition. Chang Seng-yu (late sixth century) is said to be the first artist to have been influenced by Hindu art. He introduced ink shading in his so-called 'boneless' paintings. This technique was carried on

Mantis and freesias; in search of food

through the later centuries in the painting of birds and animals and in the landscape painting of the Northern school of Li Ssu-hsün.

The artist proclaimed as the greatest master of the T'ang Dynasty was Wu Tao-tzu (born about 700) and he was renowned for his Buddhist frescoes. He is said to have painted 300 frescoes on temple walls.

The T'ang period is also credited with producing the greatest secular figure compositions and portraits. Court painters such as Yen Li-pen, Chou Fang, Chang Hsüan and Han Kan painted the more memorable social and cultural events of court life: por-

traits of emperors, young nobles and court ladies. A scroll in Boston, usually attributed to Yen Li-pen, is called *The Thirteen Emperors* and depicts emperors from the Han to the Sui Dynasty. Like *The Admonitions of the Instructress in the Palace* the theme is Confucian, with its emphasis on social stability and culture. Court painters also began to paint animals, usually horses and water buffaloes, which they saw as symbols of fiery speed and strength.

Buddhism also brought the art of flower painting into China. Buddhist banners from India were painted with flowers using a technique which Chang Seng-yu imitated. Until the T'ang period, blossoming plants, leafy bushes, small flowers and birds had been painted as decorative details in outdoor scenes. On the wall-paintings at Tunhuang, flowering plants, bushes and small flowers can be seen, interspersed among the figures. Nature painting, like landscape, was still regarded as secondary, as background to the main theme of figures and portraits, but the later T'ang period saw a gradual decline in figures and portraits and a shift in emphasis to nature, especially flower-and-bird painting. By the period of the Five Dynasties, flower-and-bird painting was the most popular art.

As for landscape painting, the traditional artist generally presented the physical world as an assemblage of forms, which were carefully analysed and depicted, and painted in the precise line technique of earlier artists such as Ku K'ai-chih (fourth century). The style was formal and decorative and often referred to as 'blue, green and gold' painting. Gold was often used better to

13

define landscape forms. This style later came to be known as the 'Northern school', a style generally used by court artists, and professionals.

Wang Wei (c.699–761), one of the greatest masters of the T'ang period, introduced a new style in landscape painting, the ink-monochrome landscape, painted in washes over an outline. Wang Wei was regarded as the founder of the 'Southern school'. The artists belonging to this school, generally scholars and amateurs, seek to represent only what is essential and to leave out unnecessary details.

SUNG AND YÜAN DYNASTIES

In China classical art means Sung art. Chinese art critics divide painting into three subject-categories: figures, landscape, and nature paintings, which include pictures of flowers and other plants, birds and insects and animals. The first category, that of figures and portraits, dominated painting until the end of the T'ang period. In the ninth century the interest of artists had begun to shift and the emphasis gradually moved from historical and figurative subjects to themes concerning nature. Two developments helped to bring about this change. First was the patronage of Emperors. Hou-chu, Emperor of Nantang (Period of Five Dynasties), patronized many great artists, among whom were Ching Hao and Kuan T'ung. It is through their influence that the typical landscape art of China was born. The patronage of Emperor Hui-tsung (Sung Dynasty) gave great impetus to the painting of birds, flowers, geese and royal park animals.

Second was the rise of the Literati school. Their concept of painting saw the end of an era for portrait and figure painting. Good portrait work stopped almost entirely during the Sung period. By the eleventh century, the shift from man to nature was so complete that even in the present day, it has not been reversed.

The painting of the Literati

The style of painting generally termed Literati had its beginning in the Sung period. This style has provided the inspiration for all scholarly painting until the present century. Su Tung-p'o (1036–1101) and his circle of intellectual friends put forward a new theory of painting known as *wen-jen hua* or Literati painting. Su Tung-p'o and his scholar-artist friends held that the aim of painting was expression, rather than accurate representation. For them, the objects and scenes served only as raw materials for the artist to express his thoughts and feelings, indeed his own very nature. His mode of expression, his ink-line and brush-stroke, revealed what kind of man he was. This theory of painting was a radical departure from the traditional view which held that a painting of an object or scene should evoke in the viewer the same thoughts and feelings as if he were actually viewing the real thing.

The Literati or scholar artists considered themselves amateur painters. They were gentlemen, poets and scholars first and artists only second. They painted in their spare time and freely experimented with styles and techniques, preferring ink on paper to colour and silk. In style and technique they departed

from orthodox styles to distinguish themselves from the professionals. Thus they painted in swift, powerful and graceful strokes, aiming to catch the essence or spirit of the object rather than a complete likeness. It is not surprising that the Literati artists confined themselves to landscape painting and the painting of flowers, birds, animals and insects, these subjects being more congenial to their artistic inclination, style and mode of presentation.

Literati landscape artists perceive landscape as a coherent vision, not as an assemblage of images. This vision draws from them an emotional response. Thus, in their compositions, they are not so much absorbed in depicting the landscape forms, as in the fusion of scene and inner emotion. A truly great Chinese landscape painting has the power to liberate our imagination and set it wandering through the mountains and valleys. Thus, the characteristic elements of the landscape art of Sung are mountains and lakes, rock pinnacles and cascading torrents emerging from the distant mists, and forest trees, especially the great pine.

The Literati artists singled out special groups of plants, which reflected their own scholarly ideals in their symbolism. The pine, and the bamboo and plum, were regarded as the 'Three Friends of Winter'. The bamboo, plum, orchid and chrysanthemum were called 'The Four Noble Plants', or 'The Four Paragons'. Each has a particular quality: the bamboo is pliant yet sturdy, remaining green in winter; the plum puts out its delicate blossoms in the snow; the fragrant orchid grows hidden in the grass, and the chrysanthe-

mum blooms in autumn when other blooms begin to wither. These qualities symbolize the scholar-recluse, a noble and dignified character maintaining his integrity in the face of adversity. The pine is also symbolic of the scholar, as a man of principles and fortitude. Because of their symbolic significance, these plant subjects were the most favoured among the Literati artists of the Sung and Yüan periods. Indeed they have maintained their eminent position as the most favoured plant subjects right through the centuries to the present day.

The seeds of the Literati style, sown in the early Sung period, grew to full maturity in the hands of the Yüan artists, especially the four great masters, Wu Chen, Huang Kung-wang, Ni Tsan and Wang Meng. Their influence has continued to the present century. They developed the texture strokes for their landscape and nature painting. To strengthen a contour or to give texture to rocks and trees they used an add-on process – richer, drier strokes over pale wet under-drawing.

The compositions of the great Literati masters were always original because their art was the genuine and spontaneous expression of an original personality. It cannot be denied that the Literati school played an extremely important role in the history of Chinese painting. It has provided the inspiration for all scholarly painting until the present day.

Eleven cranes and bamboo. A birthday greeting. The bamboo symbolizes longevity, peace and security; the crane is a bird of good augury

THE SUNG AND POST-SUNG PERIOD

The Sung period was a glorious one for flower-and-bird painting. Emperor Hui-tsung (1101–1125), the Emperor of Northern Sung, was said to be the greatest patron of art and himself a flower-and-bird artist of major rank. Two styles in flower-and-bird painting that are still popular today were introduced by two tenth-century masters, Hsü Hsi and Huang Ch'üan. Hsü Hsi introduced the Impressionistic style akin to the free use of the brush and ink technique of the Literati painters. He painted his flowers and birds swiftly in ink and ink-wash, adding only a little colour. Huang Ch'üan introduced the Realistic style, very closely related to the boneless technique of landscape painting. He painted in transparent washes of colour, laying one over the other,

*Mowtan peony and bamboo.
Symbols of prosperity, happiness
and longevity*

a style requiring precision in
brushwork, being more decorative and finely detailed.

Flower-and-bird artists of the
Yüan, Ming and Ch'ing Dynasties
followed the traditions of the
Sung period. The Ming Dynasty
re-established the Imperial Academy of Emperor Hui-tsung (Sung
Dynasty) and court artists,
following the strict rules set by
the Academy, painted in the Realistic style. The rulers of the
Ch'ing Dynasty followed the
footsteps of the Ming Emperors
and traditional standards were
strictly adhered to. However, the
Literati artists successfully developed the Impressionistic style
and this became the fashion of
the day outside the Imperial
Academy. A number of artists
combined the techniques of the

Realistic and Impressionistic styles and produced compositions of great originality. During the last hundred years, with the gradual influence of Western techniques, the emergence of two groups of artists can be observed. Artists like Ch'i Pai-shih (1863–1957), Wu Ch'ang-shih (1842–1927) and Jen Po-nien (1840–1896) kept strictly to traditional Chinese styles. Another group of artists, among them Kao Chien-fu and Tseng Yu-ho (twentieth century), combined the techniques of the East and West.

Post Yüan

The early Ming period is often referred to as the age of art scholarship. Early Ming artists were mostly content to copy the works of the old masters, particularly those of the four great masters of the Yüan. Thus, the first century of the Ming Dynasty passed without any notable developments in the Literati school. Court artists of the period, bound by the rules of the Imperial Academy, continued to paint in the Realistic tradition producing decorative compositions, rich in colour and accurate in form. During this time, Tai Chin, court artist to Emperor Hsüan-tsung, left the imperial patronage and founded a new school of landscape, known as the Che school after his native province Che Kiang. Artists belonging to the Che school followed conventions of the Southern Sung masters, academic, precise and decorative, but treated their works in an Impressionistic manner.

During the middle Ming period, the Literati tradition was re-established by Shen Chou, who founded the Wu school. The Wu artists mostly followed the styles of the four great Yüan masters, scholarly, calligraphic, free and subjective. The Wu school and Che school existed side by side until the middle of the sixteenth century. By the end of the century it became clear that the Wu school had become the dominant force in Ming painting.

Two important contemporaries of Shen Chou, the artists T'ang Yin (1479–1523) and Ch'iu Ying (1494–1552), took a position between these two divergent branches of Chinese painting as an attempt to bring about a reconciliation between the Wu and Che schools. They painted landscapes that were scholarly in content and expression yet highly professional in technique. They were also responsible for fostering a new interest in the narrative and descriptive aspects of a composition. This eased the problem of a limitation of themes faced by the Literati artists.

The early Ch'ing period (seventeenth century) found the art of the professional school; stagnant, purely decorative and without imagination and vision. Meanwhile, the Literati school split into two streams: one, called the orthodox school, consisted of artists who fully accepted the art theories of traditional Literati masters of the Sung and Yüan Dynasties, through to Shen Chou, Wen Cheng-ming and Tung Ch'i-ch'ang of the Ming Dynasty. The other consisted of artists who called themselves individualists. The individualists shared a common attitude, a refusal to be bound by rules and conventions, although their works still adhered to the Literati concept of painting. They were generally all-round artists who painted a variety of subjects in a variety of techniques. They borrowed what they pleased from the earlier masters but painted with a style and expression all their own. The leaders of the orthodox school were the so-called Six Great Masters of the early Ch'ing, Wang Shih-min, Wang Chien, Wang Hui, Wang Yüan-ch'i, (the 'Four Wangs') Wu Li and Yün Shou-p'ing. The three great individualists of the early Ch'ing were Chu Ta, K'un-ts'an (also known as Shih-ch'i) and Tao-chi (also known as Shih-t'ao). Chu Ta re-introduced the 'boneless' technique, that is, the brushstroke done entirely in wash without the use of any line.

By the eighteenth century, individualism in art became extremely popular. Some artists carried individualism to the extreme. They became so bold in their styles and presentation as to earn for themselves the label, 'Eccentric'. The most well-known are the 'Eight Eccentrics' of Yangchow. The Yangchow masters, Chin Nung and Hua Yen, can be said to have formed the last major school in traditional Chinese painting. Meanwhile, the traditions of the orthodox school of the 'Four Wangs' were being faithfully followed in the eighteenth century by the 'Four Small Wangs', Wang Su, Wang Chin, Wang Ch'en and Wang Yu.

Artistic output and development in nineteenth-century China were comparatively limited. The status of professional court artists had sunk to a low level, whilst the Literati tradition had developed to the point where styles and expressions in art had reached their boldest and freest in the hands of the 'Eccentrics'. European influence can be seen as early as the late seventeenth century, but although some court artists made great efforts to master Western shading and perspective, the Literati generally ignored European art.

From the mid-nineteenth century onwards, however, it became increasingly difficult for Chinese artists to isolate themselves from international and modern developments in Art. This culminated in the Modern Movement in Chinese Art, launched in 1916 in Canton by Kao Chien-fu. The school was called *Ling-nan p'ai*, and artists developed a style that enabled them to express contemporary subjects in traditional Chinese medium and technique. Some artists began to paint in oil on canvas, but Chinese artists living outside the People's Republic of China, especially in Taiwan, Hong Kong and Southeast Asia, continued to paint in the Chinese tradition. When abstract expressionism fired the visions of international artists elsewhere, these Chinese artists took their inspiration and painted abstract compositions of typically Chinese themes in traditional Chinese medium and technique. Meanwhile, artists in the People's Republic of China adapted themselves to the demands of a socialist society and modernization by painting contemporary subjects such as tankers or aeroplanes, an oil refinery, life in the commune, work at a construction site or in the factory. One cannot miss the ideological content and the propagandist tone in these contemporary compositions but there is evidence of a blending of traditional styles with modern ones. The traditional, however, still reigns supreme.

SYMBOLISM IN CHINESE PAINTING

There are many things to look for in a piece of Chinese painting: the composition, its vitality, the subtleties of brushwork, the perfection of form, the remarkable blending of colours and washes and tones, and many other visual aspects. In addition, to appreciate the painting fully, one must understand its symbolism.

THE FOUR PARAGON OR THE FOUR NOBLE PLANTS

Plum-blossom
The plum tree blossoms in winter. Thus it heralds the return of spring, life and hope after the end of the cycle of birth, growth and decay. It symbolizes strength, fortitude and venerable old age, and is associated with poetry and learning.

Chinese orchid
This pure and elegantly beautiful flower, whose natural habitat is secluded woodland sites, remote valleys and hidden rock crevices, symbolizes the Confucian and Taoist ideal of the noble scholar living in rural seclusion. It is also a symbol of virtue and purity.

Bamboo
The bamboo symbolizes the scholar because of its noble properties: flexible yet sturdy and evergreen. It is a symbol of longevity and of courage in adversity because it does not break even in a strong wind. As its leaves cast a welcome shade, it becomes a symbol of benevolence. Its rhizomes, besides nourishing the main stem, also send forth new shoots at close inter-

vals. Thus, it has also become a symbol of faithful performance of duty.

Chrysanthemum
The chrysanthemum blooms in autumn when other flowers begin to wither. It is therefore a symbol of the scholar and recluse. The Chinese scholar is generally depicted as a noble and dignified character living an unwordly way of life, devoted to the scholar's accomplishments of music, poetry, calligraphy and painting.

THE THREE FRIENDS OF WINTER

The Three Friends of Winter are the bamboo, plum-blossom and pine. They are so called because they stoically withstand the winter; the bamboo by its flexibility, durability and stability, as its stout stem and sturdy roots withstand the winter frost and gale, the plum-blossom by putting out its delicate blossoms in the snow, the pine by its immovable strength.

FLOWERS

Mowtan peony   the 'king of the flowers' and 'flower of riches and honour'. Symbolizes spring. It is an emblem of love and affection and a symbol of feminine beauty, also regarded as an omen of good fortune.

Plum-Blossom   symbolizes strength, fortitude and venerable old age.

Orchid – *'lan'* symbolizes spring, beauty, elegance and refinement; 'hui' symbolizes summer and the perfect human being.

Lotus   the 'superior man' among

the flowers. To the Buddhists, it is a universal symbol of purity. Symbolizes summer among the flowers of the four seasons conveying the idea of happiness and maturity.

Narcissus symbolizes purity and early spring.

Camellia signifying prosperity and long life, it heralds the Chinese New Year.

Peach Blossom known as the 'fairy fruit', and a symbol of immortality and marriage.

Magnolia symbolizes purity, feminine sweetness and beauty.

Hydrangea known as 'xiuqui hua', and a symbol of marriage.

TREES

Pine symbolizes the man of principles. Being evergreen, it is a symbol of fortitude and faithfulness.

Bamboo virtue, constancy, friendship. It is commonly known as 'Friend of China'. Also a symbol of longevity.

Plantain self-education.

Ling Chih (plant of long life) longevity and immortality.

Willow the emblem of spring, and a Buddhist symbol of meekness. Also a symbol of the fair sex owing to its beauty, suppleness and frailty.

BIRDS

A pair of Mandarin ducks conjugal fidelity.

Cock, hen and peonies. A painting to symbolize happiness and prosperity

A pair of geese marital faithfulness. The wild geese also symbolize masculine force in nature. A gaggle of wild geese symbolizes co-operation and mutual assistance.

Peacock and peahen happy marriage. The peacock also symbolizes beauty and dignity, and good fortune in business.

A pair of quails conjugal fidelity. The quail also symbolizes pugnacious courage and poverty owing to its rugged appearance.

Dove symbolizes peace.

Crane good health and longevity, also a bird of good augury.

Pheasant beauty and good fortune.

Bulbul bird these white-headed birds symbolize longevity.

Eagle heroism and keen vision and good fortune in business.

Falcon boldness and keen vision.

Swallow the messenger of success or love.

Owl the scholar and his high principles.

Cock and hen amidst rock-works in a garden of peonies they symbolize the pleasures of a country life. The cock is also an emblem of the brave soldier and faithfulness to duty.

Heron the uncorrupted Chinese official.

INSECTS

Cricket an emblem of summer and a symbol of courage.

Dragon-fly an emblem of summer, also symbolizing instability and weakness.

Lotus. Exquisite beauty and fragrance emerge unsullied from muddy waters – this flower symbolizes purity

Cranes, pine tree and plum blossom (OVERLEAF). A birthday greeting, the pine tree symbolizing longevity and the plum blossom good fortune

Cicada an emblem of autumn. Symbolizes happiness and eternal youth.

Bees symbolize diligence.

FISH

The fish symbolizes wealth and abundance; regeneration, because of its reproductive powers; and harmony, as it is seen happily swimming in its own element. A pair of fish is a sign of harmony and the joys of marriage. The carp symbolizes martial attributes because of its scaly armour and perseverance.

ANIMALS

Lion valour and felicity, illustrious offspring and wise administration.

Tiger dignity and sternness, strength and courage. Often used as a symbol of military valour.

Deer symbolizes longevity.

Dragon supreme power, the elemental forces of earth and sky.

Hare friendship and co-operation.

Goat filial piety.

Tortoise symbolizes long life.

SEAL AND INSCRIPTION

This is a vermilion 'chop' or signature wax seal stamped, usually in red, on a piece of painting or calligraphy. The simplest inscription consists of the artist's name and the date, followed by the artist's own seal. The seals of later connoissseurs of the painting could also be added. Sometimes the inscription could include the occasion for the painting and the name of the person for whom the painting was done. It could also be about the subject and style of the painting. Quite often the artist might include a piece of poetry or a literary allusion. When placing the inscription and seal, the artist makes sure that it is in an appropriate place and that it becomes an integral part of the total composition.

ABOVE LEFT *Seal*

Eagle. A symbol of heroism. The Chinese characters for 'eagle' and for 'heroism' share the same homonym, 'ying'.

Angel fish. The Chinese believe that a painting of fish will bring peace and well-being to the household

PREPARATIONS FOR PAINTING

Bees and grapes. Bees, like other insects, are a popular subject for Chinese artists, symbolizing as they do industry and diligence. Here they herald the coming of autumn, as they gather round the ripening grapes, adding life and movement to the composition

BRUSH

The brush is the instrument of all Chinese painting from the grandest academy work to the slightest sketch. The infinitely flexible and versatile Chinese brush is capable of producing all the varieties of stroke necessary to cover the full range of techniques. The Chinese brush dates back to the Neolithic period, and is stiffer than that used in the West for watercolour painting. The brush is extremely sensitive and pliable. It can be pushed back against itself in the course of a stroke without the hairs splitting or being damaged. Its tip should have a sharp point, and the bris-

The same brushstroke movement using different brushes (sizes no. 1 – no. 6)

tles should be flexible. It is important that every hair is of even length, smooth and straight. A single curly or irregular hair would destroy the appearance of strength in the stroke.

The typical Chinese brush is a carefully selected and graded bunch of hair inserted into the end of a bamboo tube. The holders are generally made of hollow bamboo reed or wood, but jade, ivory, porcelain, lacquered wood or other valuable materials are also used. The principal material for the brush head (bristles) is animal hair. Any animal hair can be used, but the most common are deer, goat, hare and wolf. For small, delicate drawings, rabbit hair is the most popular. For bold drawings, sheep hair is the best. Because of the different textures, the

brushes are generally divided into the following two categories.

HARD-HAIR BRUSH

Wolf, fox and rabbit hairs have more elasticity and offer more support in making a fine line. Hard-hair brushes can be used for both calligraphy and painting. In painting use them for line drawing and dots. A hard-hair brush with a sharp point is used for drawing and painting the veins of leaves.

SOFT-HAIR BRUSH

Brushes made from goat or sheep hair are softer and weaker. Though they are harder to control, they offer more possibilities in the variations of the brushstroke, and can create acci-

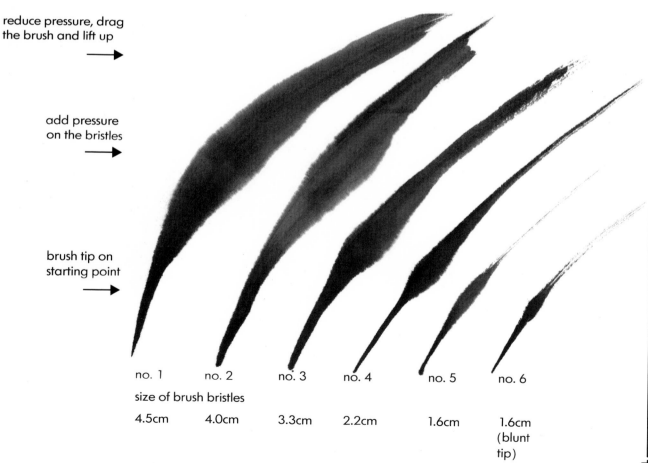

reduce pressure, drag the brush and lift up →

add pressure on the bristles →

brush tip on starting point →

| no. 1 | no. 2 | no. 3 | no. 4 | no. 5 | no. 6 |

size of brush bristles

| 4.5cm | 4.0cm | 3.3cm | 2.2cm | 1.6cm | 1.6cm (blunt tip) |

dental effects of brushwork. Soft-hair brushes are best for tinting, diluted ink-washes and thinly coloured shades.

Brushes vary in size. A bunch of bristles tied together forms the central core of the tuft, and the thickness of a brush can be increased by adding layers of covering hair to the core. Some brushes are made from a combination of plant fibres (hemp) and

Peony. King of the flowers

hair, to obtain the desired degree of softness. Plant fibres also help to hold the bristles together when the brush is saturated with water or ink.

When using a new brush, its protective glue coating must be thoroughly washed out in luke-warm water and the bristles gently loosened. The cover which comes with a new brush should be discarded, because it will not fit the head once the glue coating is washed out.

All brushes should be thoroughly washed after use. Stand the brushes in a vase or brush-case to dry.

Never throw away an old brush. Keep it for special uses, such as for impressionistic work like wrinkling and rubbing, and trim it to the required size and shape.

PAPER

Chinese painting may be done either on paper or silk. After true paper was invented (about AD 105), it quickly became favoured by artists and calligraphers because of its variety of texture and finish. It largely replaced silk fabric. The brushstroke, the essence of Chinese painting, is best shown on paper rather than silk, because silk should be treated with alum and glue before use, which makes it less absorbent.

The paper used for Chinese painting is absorbent, and so the ink diffuses as the brushstroke is laid. Different papers produce different results; some are rough and absorb ink quickly like a sponge, others have a smooth surface which resists ink. Try various kinds of paper and observe their effects before painting. In general, Chinese papers, which are usually known as rice papers in English, come in the following types:

HSUAN PAPER (UNTREATED PAPER)

Traditionally, Hsuan paper is the most commonly used for painting. Ordinary Hsuan paper is made up of two layers and is not treated with alum and glue, which makes it extremely absorbent. It is hard to control distribution of the ink or water as it runs and bleeds quickly. The paper comes in 120×60 cm (47×24 in) sheets.

COTTON PAPER (UNTREATED PAPER)

Less absorbent than Hsuan paper, cotton paper is softer and whiter. It needs less moisture

Iris and visitors. Drunk with the fragrance of summer

Ink-stick, ink-stone and ink

than the Hsuan paper. The water or ink does run but it is easily controlled if you know the paper's texture. Hsuan and cotton paper are the best for contemporary style paintings. Cotton paper comes in sheet sizes 120 × 60 cm (47 × 24 in) and 142 × 78 cm (56 × 31 in).

HALF-MATURED PAPER

This paper is half-raw and half-treated. It is less absorbent, but the ink does run and bleed as the brushstroke is laid, but very slowly. It is the paper to use when you wish to do a piece of painting in both contour and contemporary styles. One side of the paper is smoother than the other, and that is the side for painting. Half-matured paper comes in rolls or sheets, depending on your preference.

MATURED PAPER

This paper has been specially treated. It is the least absorbent and is therefore the best paper for contour-style painting. This paper can be bought in rolls of different widths or in sheets, and can be cut to the size you require.

INK

Chinese black ink, which dates back to the later Han Dynasty, is the formal media for both calligraphy and painting. An ink-stick and ink-stone are necessary to produce the ink, or alternatively liquid-ink is available.

INK-STICK

The ink is made from the soot of burnt pine-wood mixed with a little gum, and moulded into ink-sticks of varying shapes and

sizes. The most popular is the rectangular block bar. An ink-stick usually has letterings on it, showing the trade name, and is often embossed with calligraphic decoration, usually an animal or landscape design. Old ink-stick is believed to be good, but it cracks very easily, due to the heat and air-conditioning in a dry climate. The superiority of liquid Chinese ink lies in its delicate, fine and smooth colour tone. It is transparent and waterproof, becoming permanent once used on the paper. Chinese ink will last for centuries without fading.

INK-STONE

The ink-stone dates back to the late Han Dynasty. It is carved out of a slate-like rock, and is a black, flat stone with a shallow depression in the middle where the ink is ground. At one end of the ink-stone is a 'well' for

Colour

water. The ground ink flows into this well and mixes with the water. The size of the ink-stone varies, depending on personal preference. For ordinary use, most people choose the small one. Calligraphers and painters need larger ones for they need more freshly ground ink. If your ink-stone is too small to grind all the ink you require at a time, it is necessary to grind more and pour the extra fluid into a little cup with a lid. Cover it so it will not evaporate.

Use a smaller ink-stone if you are doing just a small piece of painting on that day. The ink will evaporate if it is not continuously used, and you need to wash your ink-stone once the ink has dried. Use a bigger ink-stone if you are doing a painting which needs a bigger brush and more ink. To be on the safe side, grind

more than you usually expect to use: ink that is ground again is different in concentration and tone compared with freshly ground ink. This difference usually results in a noticeable variation in tone and thickness on your paper. It is wise to make fresh ink for each piece of painting. Not only does old ink turn an unpleasant brownish colour, it also tends to dry up into a gum-like consistency, making the ink flow harshly and unevenly over the paper.

After use, just wash your ink-stone under running water. Take care not to drop it as it will crack and break. After grinding the ink, do not leave the ink-stick on the ink-stone. The extra-strong glue of the ink-stick will cause it to stick to the stone and when the stick is removed a sliver of the ink-stone slate may be pulled out, which will ruin the smooth surface of the ink-stone. The

quality of the ink-stone is just as important as that of the ink-stick. It will take you a long time to grind the ink if the surface is too smooth, but if it is too coarse the surface is too rough to produce fine ink.

HOW TO GRIND THE INK

Chinese ink is water-soluble. The ink is produced by grinding the ink-stick in some water against the ink-stone. Drop several drops of water on the flat surface of the ink-stone, use the ink-stick and grind firmly in a circular motion. You need to apply quite a lot of pressure to grind the ink off the stick. If you put too much pressure into the grinding, coarse ink is produced. But if the pressure is too light, it may take you a long time to produce ink of the right consistency. Experience will help your technique.

Brush, brush holder, brush rest, paper weight and dish. Brushes with brown bristles are hard-hair, those with white bristles are soft-hair

Hold the ink-stick upright and flat against the stone. With a firm and steady grip, rub the ink-stick back and forth or in a circular motion. While grinding, hold the side of the ink-stone with your left hand to prevent the ink-stone from moving. During the grinding, you can see that the ink gradually becomes thicker. As a general guide, the ink is ready for use when the ink-stick leaves a dry trace on the ink-stone while you make the grinding motion. It is best to test it with your brush on the paper. If the ink is too thick it will not run freely on the paper. If it is too thin, it will blot and expand into thicker lines than you intend to draw.

COLOUR

For Chinese colour painting, watercolour is used. Watercolours are commonly used for washes and tinting after the ink has been applied. Colour may be used alone or mixed with ink. There are two groups of colours, one obtained from plants and the other from minerals. Indigo, gamboge and saf-flower red are obtained from plants. Red ochre, vermilion, azurite, malachite green and flake white are mineral pigments. They are available in small solid pieces in pasteboard boxes or in powder form in little packets or bottles. Small mortars or pestles are used for grinding powdered colours into a smooth consistency. Add a little water before grinding.

Chinese colour sticks can now be purchased and ground on a grey stone, in much the same way as the ink-stick. Colours come in small tin-boxes or tubes.

Watercolour must not be used directly on absorbent paper. Mix the paint with a little water to the correct consistency for each individual stroke. You can load not just one colour, but two or three colours at one time, on the Chinese brush. This is why it is best to use a large dish or saucer instead of a Chinese dish or palette. Take out the colours you intend to mix and put them at the edge of the saucer. Add a little water and mix your colours to the tone or shade you desire. As a beginner, you can practise with ordinary watercolours.

OTHER ITEMS

Apart from the four essentials described above, the following items are necessary.

Brush holder a cylindrical container to hold the brushes is useful. Chinese ones are usually made from porcelain, bamboo or pottery.

Brush rest often shaped like a mountain peak or a camel's hoof. It is useful for resting the brush while you are painting. You can use a dinner plate for this purpose.

Small water container holds the clean water for grinding the ink. It is usually 10 cm (4 in) in diameter and made of porcelain, and it comes with a small brass spoon. You can, however, use a cup instead.

Brush washer a porcelain dish normally circular or rectangular in shape, 5 cm (2 in) high and 20 cm (8 in) in diameter. You may use any deep bowl or cup for this purpose, and you will probably need several for each painting session.

Carps in the lily pond. The lily emerges unsullied by the muddy water. The leaping carp was often used as an allusion to passing the Imperial Examination

Paper weight you will find this necessary to hold the painting paper flat and in place. Place the paper weights near the top edges of your paper before starting to paint.

Cloth or blotting paper the Chinese paper used for painting and writing that absorbs the ink from the brushstrokes. Lay out a piece of cloth or blotting paper under the painting paper to absorb the water that may go through the paper during the painting.

33

Otherwise, the ink will seep back into the painting paper. The best materials for this purpose are black felt or wool. Newspapers or underlying wallpaper can also be used. Whenever you need to move your painting paper, you should move both painting paper and blotting paper (or cloth) together, or else the wet spots on the blotting paper will form blotches on other parts of your painting paper.

Dish (palette) a dish used as a palette for mixing the colour/ink for different tones. Any kind of dish or saucer is ideal for mixing, as you can put the colour at the edge of the saucer, and mix the colour tone in the centre.

Newspaper or underlying wallpaper ideal for beginners to practise their strokes, since it is inexpensive and always available. The absorbent quality of these papers is fairly poor. However, once you master your brushwork you can easily adjust your brushstrokes to the more absorbent Hsuan (rice) paper.

Peacock and peahen. Signifying a happy marriage, and also prosperity in business, the pair of birds are complemented perfectly by the backdrop of wisteria

PRELIMINARY TECHNICAL STUDIES

HOLDING THE BRUSH

The brush is held by the thumb, index and middle finger. The ring finger and small finger play their part as well, although they do not actually hold the brush.

STEPS TO FOLLOW

a Pick up a brush between your thumb and index finger.

b Gently place the pad of your thumb on the left side of the brush handle. Allow the upper part of the handle to lean on the second knuckle joint of your index finger.

c Place the soft pads of your index finger and middle finger on the right side of the handle.

d Your ring finger should now be supporting the brush from behind.

e Your little finger is not in contact with the brush at all, but it is positioned right behind the ring finger and gives support to the ring finger.

Your thumb and index finger keep the handle in place and use pressure from the arm to apply the stroke. The middle and ring finger do the work of turning, twisting and moving. Although the little finger does not directly touch the brush, it is a conductor as well as a supporter – it draws the ring finger along. While drawing a delicate line or stroke, it gives support to the stroke.

Your finger grip should be firm and well balanced, and you should hold the brush away from the palm. This gives your brush-work freedom and control. At the same time, relax your hand, arm and entire body. In fact,

your palm should be so flexible that if you positioned your hand at wrist level, you could draw a circle 15–20 cm (6–8 in) in diameter without moving your elbow or arm.

A firm but relaxed hold produces rugged, severe, powerful strokes. A looser hold results in a graceful and tender stroke.

If your hold is too tight, your fingers will be squeezed tightly and your whole hand will close into a fist. If your small finger

Handling the brush, step by step from (a) to (e). Correct handling (fig e) – the wrist is relaxed and there is a hollow space between the thumb and other fingers. Incorrect handling (fig f) – the wrist shows a folding of the skin and the thumb is pressed tight against the palm and fingers

touches the centre of the palm, your hold is too tight. While painting, you need to apply rolling, twisting and turning strokes. With this tight hold, the brush cannot perform effectively and freely. Also, your fingers can get tired and cramped after a short while.

WHERE TO HOLD THE BRUSH

The length of a brush varies – the bigger the bristles, the longer the brush handle. When you hold the brush higher up you can execute more movements with the brush. This is the reason for having a longer handle for the big brush which is used for large, free-flowing strokes. If your hold is lower down nearer the bristles, the stroke is heavy

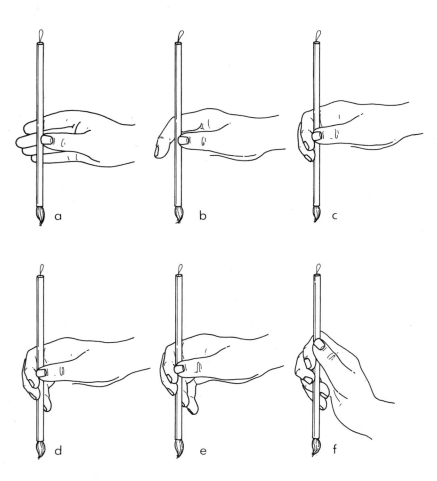

Bamboo and sparrows. A painting to greet the new year

and your brushstroke movements are limited to rolling, twisting, turning and rubbing. The movement appears stiff.

The fine small brush has a shorter handle. If you hold this brush very low down, you can manipulate it for fine and meticulous detail.

The way you hold your brush as well as the level of your wrist should not change, no matter what brushstrokes you wish to do.

Raising your wrist and elbow above the paper enables you to execute free and spontaneous brushstrokes, suitable for a large painting in contemporary style. You may rest your wrist lightly on the table while doing a small painting in contour style, especially when you need to do delicate outlines.

CALLIGRAPHY

Ancient Chinese words were hieroglyphs consisting of pictures and figures of concrete objects. From about the second century AD, characters were written with a brush in ink on silk or paper. The Chinese character has always retained its original basic meaning or ideas.

Throughout the centuries, training in calligraphy has always involved the same characters, the same sorts of brushes and ink, and the same methods. The order in which the strokes of a character are written is absolutely fixed. The calligrapher must maintain a sense of spacing and balance in the strokes. He must concern himself with the texture of the ink, and the power and flexibility of the strokes he produces. The aim is to produce a composition of great beauty and sensitivity with its own vibrating spirit. Without doubt, calligraphy in itself is an art form of the highest level. Some Chinese place calligraphy on a higher level than ink-painting.

WHY PRACTISE CALLIGRAPHY?

The essence of Chinese painting is contained within 'brush control'. Skill comes only with constant practice, concentration and discipline. You will know that you have mastered the skill when brushworks and brush movements become instinctive; when the appropriate positions to take, the correct pressure to apply and the speed of the stroke all come naturally. Calligraphy is an ideal way for a beginner in Chinese painting to practise brush handling, brushstrokes and brush movements. The techniques are the same. Calligraphy can be practised at any time you wish. Just pick up a brush and write a character, which is actually a series of beautiful strokes, and you can gaze at your calligraphic creation with pleasure. As for a good painting, you have to wait for inspiration – another thing all together!

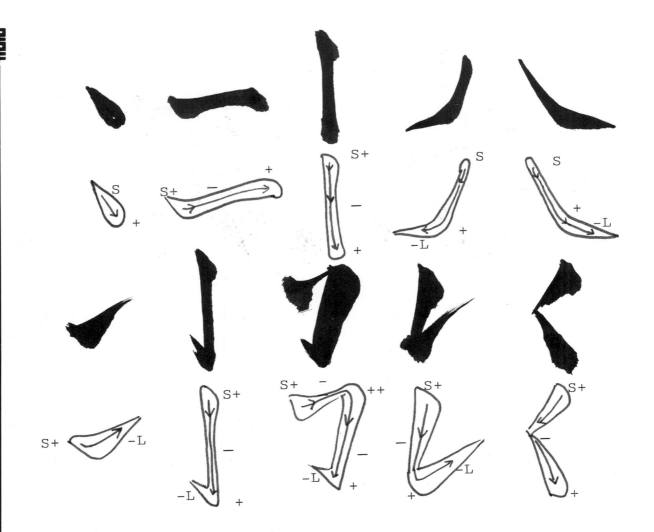

The various brush movements used for calligraphy. Hold the brush upright and with the tip pointing at S follow the direction of the arrows: lift up the brush at L. You may apply pressure or decrease pressure on the bristles while you make a brush stroke.

Key:
S   brush tip pointed down
+   apply pressure
+ +   apply more pressure
—   decrease pressure
L   lift up brush

COPYING AND TRACING FOR PRACTICE

Copying and tracing the works of an old master is useful for beginners but it may become a bad habit eventually. Once you have mastered the brushworks and brush movements you should learn to create your own personal brush styles.

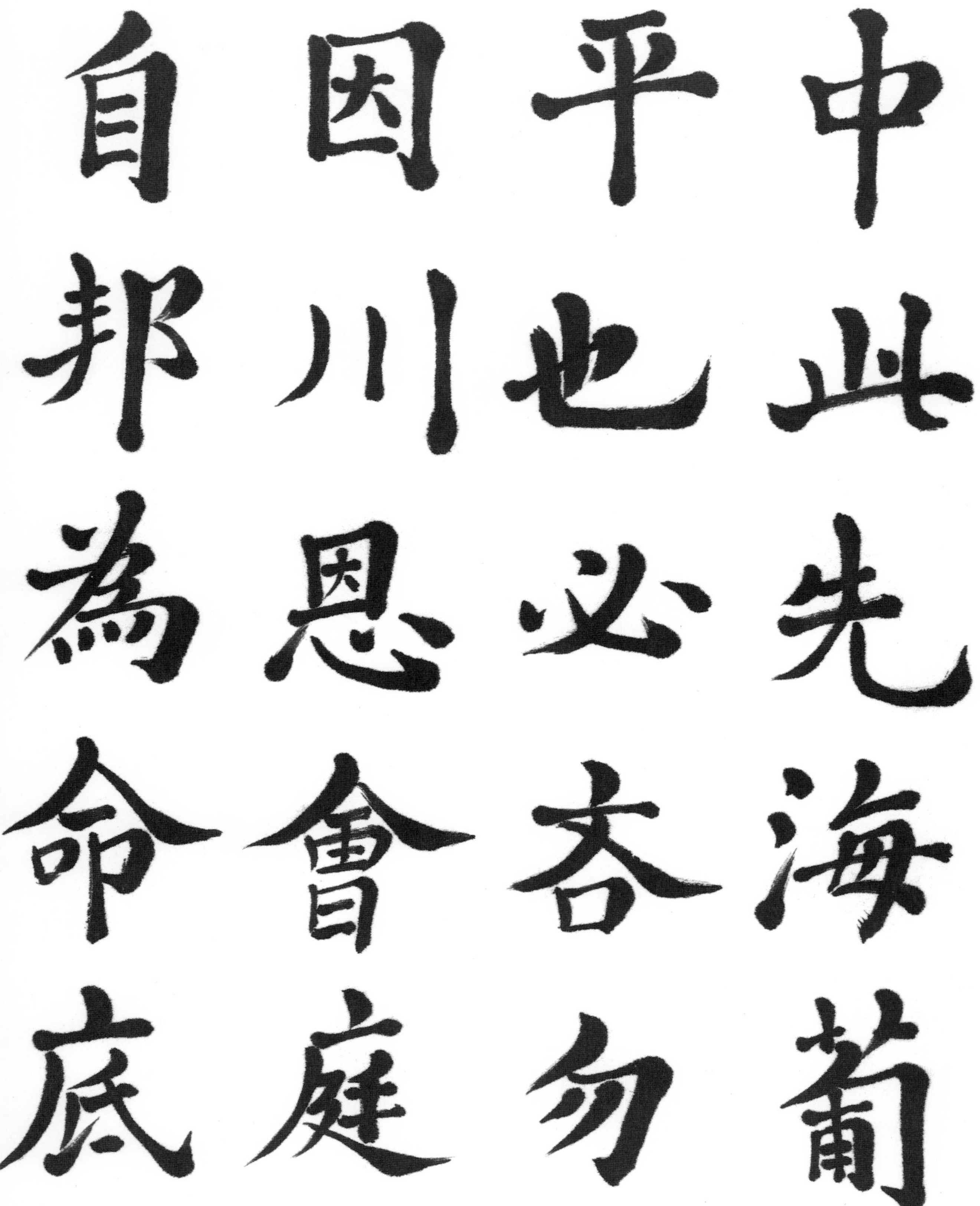

中 平 因 自
此 也 川 邦
先 必 恩 為
海 吞 會 命
葡 勿 庭 底

Some Chinese characters for copying and tracing for practice

BRUSHWORK TECHNIQUES IN PAINTING

BASIC CATEGORIES OF BRUSHWORK

I Centre brush
Hold the brush upright, bringing the tip down in the middle of the stroke.

II Side brush
Hold the brush at an angle to produce thicker strokes. The larger the number of bristles used against paper, the thicker the stroke.

III Turning brush
Twist the brush suddenly to change the line direction.

IV Rolling brush
While using the side brush-stroke, you can roll over your brush and thus change the direction of a brush movement. Holding the brush at an angle (as in the side brushstroke), roll the brush back on itself to change line direction.

V Pressing and lifting
Holding the brush upright, press the tip on the paper to make a broad stroke. Half-lift the brush with only the tip touching the paper to make a swift, thin line.

VI Dragging and pushing
Hold the brush in an upright or oblique position to draw a line with a dragging or pushing stroke.

VII Wrinkling and rubbing
Having loaded the brush with charred ink, hold it obliquely and rub it over the paper.

Centre brush

Side brush, showing the effects of loading and pressure

Turning brush

Rolling brush

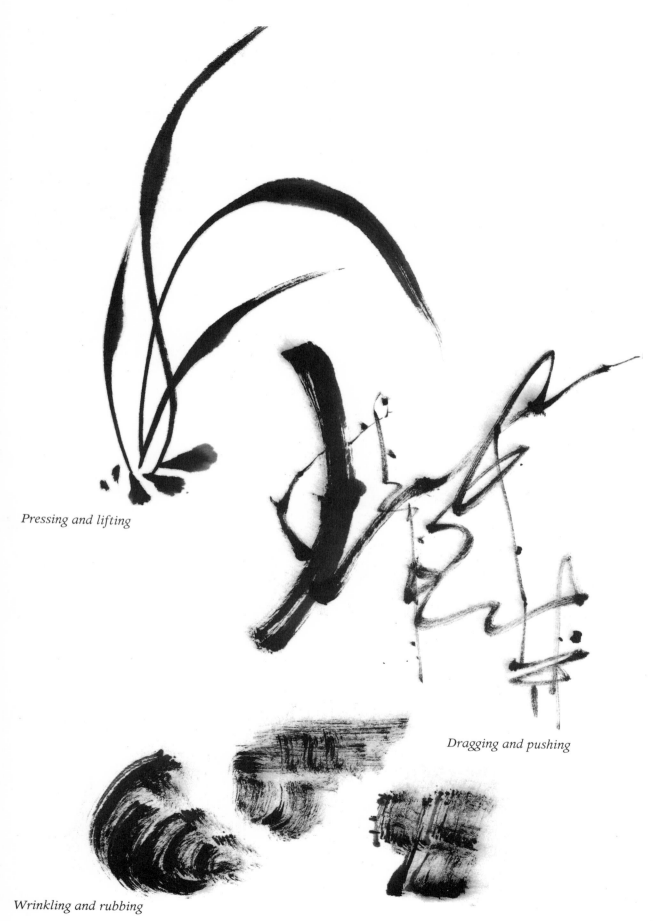

Pressing and lifting

Dragging and pushing

Wrinkling and rubbing

Nine fishes. The homonym which exists between 'yu' meaning fish and 'yu' meaning abundance, is put to effective use to convey a new year wish for everlasting happiness, good fortune and abundant wealth

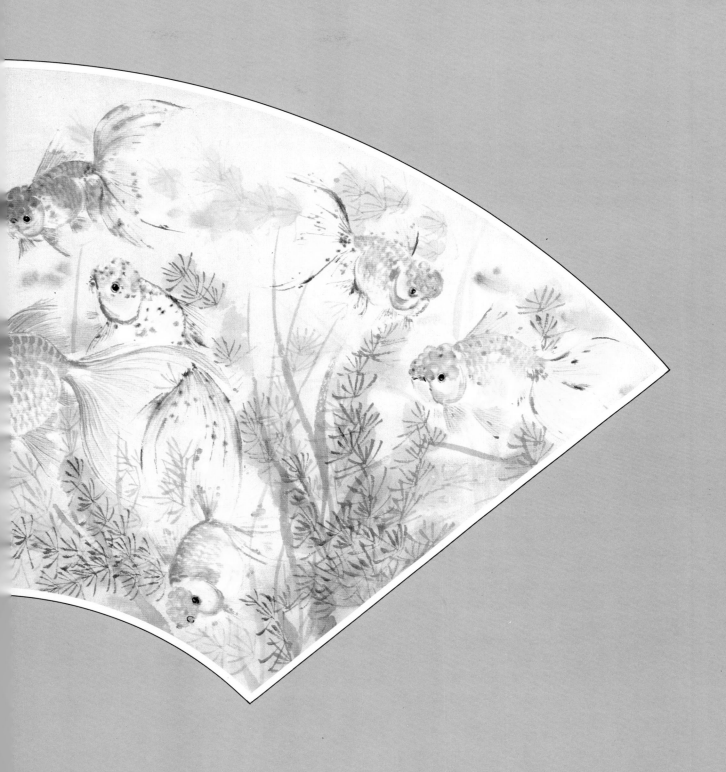

BRUSH CONTROL

Chinese artists try to make their pictures as alive as possible. This vitality, the feeling for life, comes from the sense of movement in the brushstroke which is the basis of all Chinese paintings. An artist's brushstroke depends on brush control. Moisture, pressure and speed are the three essentials to bear in mind.

Moisture

The moisture in the brush should be one of your main concerns before putting brush to paper. The amount of water you wish to load depends on what effect you want. You must also bear in mind the absorbency of the paper.

Pressure

How broad or slender a stroke is depends on the pressure of the bristles on the paper. The broader the line or brushstroke (whether upright or oblique), the heavier the pressure should be.

To exert the right pressure for each brushstroke is a difficult feat. You need to restore the elasticity to the bristles after you have applied pressure. You also need to be in full control when changing pressure while manipulating a particular stroke movement.

Speed

Different speeds create different textures. A steady speed produces a firm and strong line or stroke. If the brush moves too fast, the result is a weak and fuzzy stroke. If the brush moves too slowly, the stroke will be out of shape because the ink will run and bleed under a hesitant movement.

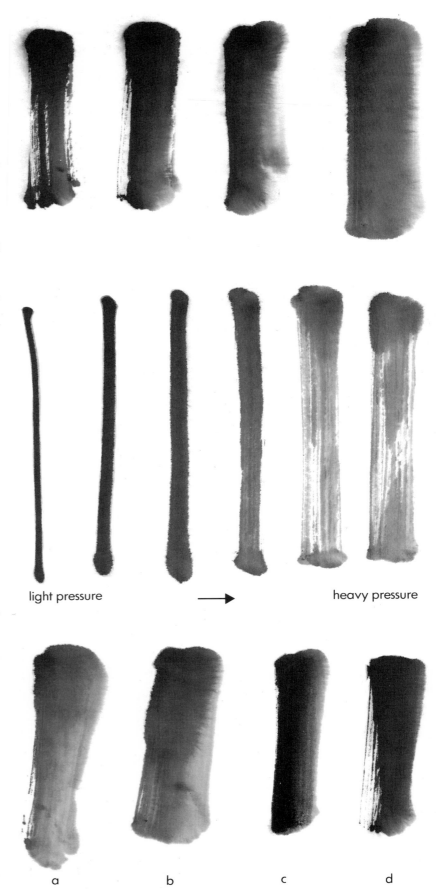

light pressure   →   heavy pressure

a   b   c   d

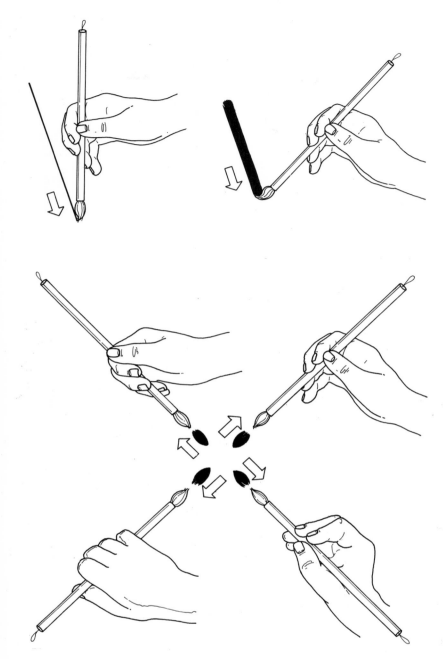

HOW TO APPLY THE BRUSH

Upright position

Always hold the brush perpendicular to the paper, either halfway up the handle or lower down for small and detailed work; or higher up for the larger strokes. Depending on the pressure applied, you can obtain strokes of varying thickness, shape and tone.

This upright brush position is always used for calligraphy, for painting in contour style, for delicate fine lines, for broader strokes and also for dotting.

If only the tip touches the paper lightly, the stroke will be a thin one. If pressure is applied, the stroke will become broader because more of the bristles are used.

The tone of the stroke depends on the amount of ink or colour loaded on the bristles. When the tip alone is in contact with the paper, only one tone is obtained. When pressure is added, a second tone appears.

Oblique position

This position allows more of the bristles to come into contact with the paper. The tip and the upper bristles move parallel to each other. When you hold the brush in a slant position, it gives you more freedom and flexibility in your brushstroke movements. The effect of your brushstroke movements depends on the following factors.

- loading (dry, moist, wet)
- tone (light, medium, dark; one tone, two-tone or three-tone)
- pressure (light, moderate, heavy)
- speed (slow, moderate, quick)
- angle of slant (generally varying from 10 to 80 degrees)

TOP LEFT *Loading the brush. From left to right: dry, moist, wet, very wet*

CENTRE LEFT *Pressure, using a no. 3 brush, upright position*

BOTTOM LEFT *Speed*
a   *speed uneven*
b   *too slow*
c   *right speed and pressure – wet-loading*
d   *right speed and pressure – dry-loading*

TOP *Upright and oblique positions*

IMMEDIATELY ABOVE *Oblique position. The various ways of holding the brush for movements in different directions*

Different combinations of the above factors produce different brushstrokes. Thus, this position can produce a multitude of breathtaking brushstrokes that never ceases to surprise and excite.

The oblique position is always used for contemporary-style painting.

PAINTING STYLES

Chinese techniques of painting are centuries old and have been handed down from one master to another. There are only two main painting styles.

Contour style (out-lining style)

The contour style is one where lines are used to suggest form and texture. Contours, may be outlined in light ink and later reinforced with darker ink. Alternatively, ink washes may be applied after the outlines have dried. This method can also be used to provide the structural foundation for a colour composition. Dimension and details are later added by applying colour washes.

This style is ideal for beginners. It demands a steady hand movement and calls for a thorough analysis of the structure of the objects to be painted. The contour style artist strives for realistic, almost photographic, likeness.

Contemporary style (non-outlining)

This style needs fewer brushstrokes. Thus a contemporary style painting can be completed very quickly; a painting of peony blossoms can be done in a few minutes. In order to achieve a harmonious effect, all the strokes should be finished before they dry. This is to ensure that the strokes blend together. Contemporary uses colour and ink, unlike the monochrome style of contour.

Many artists make use of both styles in the same painting. The strong contour-style ink work is combined with the free-flowing spontaneous strokes of contemporary style, usually applied in colour. The powerful lines of ink are set off by subtle colour washes to produce works of art that give an immediate feeling of life, growth and movement.

BELOW *Painting styles*
a   *contour style (outlining style)*
b   *contemporary style (non-outlining style)*

OPPOSITE *The dazzle of summer blossoms*

a

b

47

Shades of ink

PRINCIPAL WAYS OF USING INK

Handling the ink is as important as the art of wielding the brush. Without any special technique, the ink in the brush would be evenly blended, and would produce an even colour on the paper, flat, static and toneless. Tonal colour and texture are essential to a picture's vibrancy and life.

Shades of ink

When diluted with water, ink can be made to produce many different shades. Generally there are seven: charred, deep dark, dark, medium, light, very light and pale. Charred ink is very black, thick and cream-like. To prepare it, stir the ink-stick in water on the ink-stone until the ink is cream-like in consistency. Gradually add water to charred ink to obtain the various shades ranging from deep dark to very pale – the more water, the lighter the shade.

Side-ink technique

The action consists of just one upright brushstroke, which gives tonal effect to the line. Rinse the brush in a light tone, and if the brush is wet, draw out the excess water. Dip one side of the brush in darker ink and immediately draw the line, straight, twisting or rolling with an upright brush-stroke. The result is a line which is darker on one side and lighter on the other. This gives a three-dimensional effect.

After dipping the brush in the ink, you must use the brush at once. This is because the dark ink will start to run within the brush and if left too long, the ink will become completely blended.

Spilled-ink technique

This requires no outlining. Wet the brush and apply with a broad, full stroke in one quick movement.

Spilled-ink technique

Side-ink technique

Layer technique

This technique is used almost exclusively for painting land-scapes. It involves covering an area in the painting layer by layer. After the first light layer of ink is dry, tint another darker layer over it. Later, add another darker layer. Apply several layers. Finally, highlight with black dots and lines.

Layer technique

Heavy-ink technique

Use a fairly dry brush loaded with thick dark ink. Dot on rocks or branches. This tech-nique is used for touching up a picture to accentuate planes and contours.

Heavy-ink technique

Water consistency for a scorched, moist or wet effect

To achieve a vigorous and vital effect, not only is the tone important, but also the amount of the water in the brush. Depending on the water content, a brushstroke may look scorched, moist or wet.

Make the brush very dry if you want a sear stroke; add a little water for a moist stroke; and more for a wet stroke.

Ink-washes

Mix the ink and water in a clean saucer to the desired tone. Load a large brush with plenty of water, and apply to the rice paper spontaneously, so that the wash does not spread too much on the paper. Different shades may be obtained with each application. Try to prevent the wash from spreading beyond the outline by making sure the outline is dry before you apply the ink-wash.

Scorch, moist, wet effect

Ink-wash

Dark ink on light ink-washes

This technique makes the painting look rich and moist. First, apply light ink-washes on the paper. Immediately apply deep dark brushstrokes while the paper is still wet to merge the two colours.

Dark ink on light ink-wash

PRINCIPAL WAYS OF USING COLOUR

Colour-loading is an effective technique that is only possible with the specialized Chinese brush. With the same colour, differently loaded and using the various brushstrokes techniques, it is possible to achieve the most contrasting effects in colour intensity and tone. Such skills can only come with practice and experience. The varieties of brushstroke are quite unlimited. The brush can be applied upright, oblique, twisting or rolling. When using more than one colour, it is very important to achieve a well-blended mix of colours in one single stroke. When the moisture and tone are just right and the brushstroke is skilfully manipulated with the right pressure and speed, the result is magical.

Contour style

First outline the contour in a light ink or colour. In a saucer, add a little water and mix the colour to the shade you require. Stir well with the brush. Use no. 1 or 2 brush, and when the ink/colour outline is dry, apply the colour-washes within the contoured area, the same way as you apply the ink-wash.

Contour style in colour

Layer technique

This is used almost exclusively for landscapes. The bold brush-stroke combined with this particular method of using colour, wonderfully captures the vibrant beauty of nature. If several layers of colour are needed, wait for the previous layers to dry before applying an additional darker layer.

Two- or three-tone technique

It is best to use a medium or large brush whose bristles are packed quite thickly, ideal for loading. First, make sure that the colour to be used is mixed well to the tone you want. Load the brush with lighter colour and then gently scrape the top section of the brush on the edge of the saucer to let out excess water. Gently roll the tip of the brush in the darker colour. Allow the colour to rise into the bristles. As it rises from the tip, it will gradually become diluted by the water in the brush. Finally, dip the tip of the brush in the darkest colour. Now the brush is loaded with three tones of colour.

You should vary the positions of the three-tone brush and the portion of the bristles used to create a brushstroke of varying broadness and tone. If you apply your brush in an upright position, only the bristles at the tip of the brush will be in contact with the paper, and only one tone will appear on the paper. If you apply the brush in a slightly slanting position, only half of the brush will come into contact with the paper and thus two of the tones will be used. When broadness of stroke, is desired, as

Layer technique

Two- or three-tone

well as different tones, load the brush with only two colours.

For a three-colour-tone, apply the brush in one broad oblique stroke. The whole brush will come into full contact with the paper and the result is a beautifully blended three-tone brushstroke.

If the brush becomes too dry, slightly immerse the side of the brush in the lighter tone saucer. Use your own judgement when you need to re-load. Wash the brush completely before re-loading.

IMPORTANT CONSIDERATIONS BEFORE COMMENCING A PAINTING

COMPOSITION

What we look for in a Chinese painting is not only a work of art, but also the rhythmic vigour of each stroke and of the whole composition. Chinese paintings are far less detailed than most Western paintings, and therefore a state of balance in the design is important. Devote yourself first to composing each component part of the picture well, and then to arranging the parts into the design of the whole. Never try to make an exact copy of nature, but create a world of nature of your own. Adjust the positions of the components in a composition to the size and shape of the painting. The spaces that separate the various components are part of the design. Balance is essential. The artist must be able to convey the essence of the subject in a few single strokes and give an immediate feeling of life, growth and movement. The natural world comes into rhythmic life through the Chinese brushstroke and the dynamic equilibrium in the painting.

LIGHT

It is best to paint by daylight. Early morning has always been regarded as the best time for painting; when the creative mind is fresh, inspiration comes easier and the morning light is just right. Also you will get enough time to finish your painting before dark. It is advisable to stop your painting before dark. Artificial lighting not only hinders the making of beautiful strokes but results in a noticeable difference in their tone, colour and thickness.

Organize your pictorial composition well before you start. If it is a large painting, which you cannot finish in one working day, you should separate the various components and do one at a time. For instance, paint the flower blossoms in one day, the birds the next, and the leaves on another day. This makes it easier to achieve a harmonious effect. If you paint flower blossoms on different days, it will be impossible to retrieve the same pressure and speed of the different brushstrokes, colour tones and thicknesses.

POSTURE

Chinese painting can be done in a standing or sitting position, depending on your personal preference. When painting in a standing position, you should co-ordinate your body movement with your brushstroke movement, and give more strength and freedom to your arm, especially when painting large objects, such as lotus leaves, and landscape in ink-washes.

When doing a painting in contemporary style, a standing position allows more freedom and gives you the strength you need for your brushstrokes. It gives you a better perspective on the whole painting, especially if it is a big piece.

For a contour-style painting, a sitting position is preferred. The elaborate subject and mechanical line-drawing need a slow and steady hand. A sitting position gives your hand good and firm support. Whether you choose the standing or sitting position, your body should form an immobile base. The shoulder initiates the movement by leading the arm, and the arm leads the hand that holds the brush. The whole body is actually doing the painting, not just the fingers. Bend your left elbow naturally and rest your left hand on the paper to hold it like a paper-weight. Do not incline or bend the body or move it about while painting. The slightest movement can upset the focus of the eye and impede the control of the arm. During the brush movement, you should shift your body weight to co-ordinate with the arm-and-hand movement.

Wisteria. A fascinating contrast — the stout bamboo stem and the creeping vine

COPYING FOR PRACTICE

To learn Chinese painting, one must start by imitating the works of the masters. Through a series of unsuccessful attempts, eventually you will find that you are able to manipulate the brush, gradually producing your own creations. Thus, imitation is very important training. To paint from memory is another important practice. After close observations of life and nature forms, the habits of growth, and the effects of seasonal changes, you will have your own ideas to express, and can develop a personal style.

4

CHINESE PAINTING TECHNIQUES

Mowtan peonies and pheasants. The birds of beauty and good fortune in the midst of the flowers of riches and honour, which are also emblems of love and affection. A painting which celebrates the joys of marriage

GRASSES

Before you try to compose a painting of your own, it is important to know the principles of nature. Grasses, for example, may be very different from one another, and so varying amounts of water, brushstrokes and ink/colour tones will be employed to depict them in different environments.

In spring, the grasses are young and tender. They are thick and exuberant in summer. They wither in autumn and dry up in winter. For a colour composition, use moist greenish yellow or a blue-green tone for spring and summer grasses. Use brownish yellow-green or orange-red for grasses in autumn and winter.

It is important to note that when a grass blade appears upside down, lighter tones should be applied for the underside of the blade. If stems are shown, paint the stems first and then the blades. Paint ears or flowers last. The techniques for painting the various types of grasses are shown below.

YOUNG GRASS

Use a no. 3 or 5 brush for long upward strokes. The movement is similar for painting orchid leaves. Vary the directions of the strokes and group them in patches. As you brush upwards, slightly increase the pressure at the centre of the stroke.

DRY GRASS

Use a no. 5 brush dry-loaded. Apply upright brushstrokes to form the grass-stalks in varying directions. Then, with the tip of the brush held upright, make quick outward movements to form the grass blades.

Young grass

Dry grass

TENDER GRASS

i Use a no. 4 brush, moist-loaded in medium tone. With the tip of an upright brush, make quick downward strokes. Vary the directions of the strokes and group them in patches.

ii With the tip of an upright brush, make simple downward strokes. Vary the directions and also group them in patches.

iii Use a no. 4 brush moist-loaded in medium tone. Apply quick upright brushstrokes to form grass-stalks in varying directions. Short, curved strokes are added to each grass-stalk. Point the tip of an upright brush towards the stalk, press slightly and make a quick stroke, gradually releasing the pressure towards the tip of the blade.

iv Use a no. 4 brush moist-loaded in medium tone. With the tip of an upright brush make simple downward strokes increasing pressure as the brush moves down.

MOSS GRASS

For moss grasses, use wet brush strokes and group them in patches.

i Use a no. 4 brush wet-loaded in one or two tones. With the tip of an upright brush, starting at the base, make quick outward strokes. Occasionally add a little pressure.

ii Each unit consists of four–five dots. Use the tip of an upright brush, press down and then release the pressure while directing the stroke towards the group and forming a fan shape.

iii For round dot moss, hold the brush upright and dot the paper. The dots' size depends on the pressure applied on the paper.

Four examples of tender grass

Three examples of moss grass

WEED

i This is done in the same way as moss grass (ii), only it consists of more than nine leaves and it forms a circular pattern instead of a fan shape.

ii Same as above. Use a no. 4 brush dry-loaded in medium tone, and add in the stems. Make quick outward dragging movements.

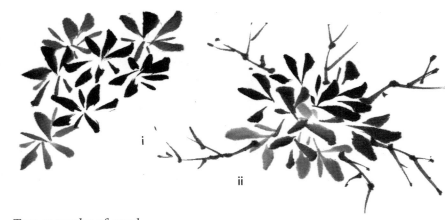

Two examples of weed

ROCKS

A Chinese painter paints rocks with varying strokes and tones to express the dimension, form, texture and character of the rock. The following steps illustrate how a rock is painted.

OUTLINE

Use a no. 2 or 3 brush, dry-loaded in light tone, to outline the form of the rock. Use upright brushstrokes, starting at the lower left side of the rock and working up towards the top, then over the top. Use oblique brushstrokes down the right side to the base. Apply a darker tone over it. To show the irregularity, vary the pressure. As you paint, you may press or roll the brush gently between your fingers making breaks in certain places according to the form of the rock.

INTERIOR STROKES

Use a no. 1 or 2 brush, dry-loaded in medium tone. With an oblique brushstroke apply wrinkling strokes. Add a darker tone over it when the patch is dry. With the tip of an oblique brushstroke make quick downward movements. The base of the rock should not be done in a straight,

outlining

wrinkling

washing
Steps in painting a rock

dotting

APPLICATION OF WASHES

This is a step to add more tonal variation to the rock. Use a no. 1 or 2 brush, wet-loaded in a light tone, and apply quick oblique strokes. Colour-washes may be applied instead of the ink-washes; grey-blue or red-ochre is used to wash over the lighter parts. Then, apply indigo or dark-blue to the shaded parts while they are still wet. This is done so that the two colours will blend naturally.

horizontal line. Apply one or more brushstrokes to join up the uneven vertical fissures at the base. The wrinklings must always be slightly overlapping to show the texture.

MOSS DOTS

After the basic structure of the rock has been clearly delineated, moss dots may be added before or after the washes. To show moss or weeds that may grow on the rock, use an upright brush, add dots in light ink, in irregular and slightly over-lapping groups. While the light-toned dots are still wet, add dots in charred or dark ink to give more accent to the rock wrinkles.

Different ways to paint rocks

bamboo

wisteria

peach blossom

willow

*Leaves formed with one
brushstroke*

Chinese orchid

62

LEAVES

The leaf is the plant's chief organ of food production. Leaves are generally attached to a stalk or petiole, on which they adopt characteristic positions and grow to a fixed size. The leaves which are often displayed in Chinese paintings are shown in this section in contemporary styles.

LEAVES FORMED WITH ONE BRUSHSTROKE

The long grass-like leaf of the orchid and day-lily, and the short curved leaf of the willow and wisteria, fall into this category.

The long grass-like leaf is painted with a single stroke of varying pressure, swooping upward from the base of the plant (use a no. 1 or 2 brush). Hold the brush upright and, using the tip of the brush, move it along gradually, adding pressure to achieve variations of width in the brushstroke. Lift the brush towards the end of the stroke. To add life and movement to the long slender blade of the leaf, hold the brush in an upright as well as an oblique position when applying a single brushstroke.

The short curved leaf is painted with a short, single brushstroke. Use the tip of an upright brush to press slightly, gradually releasing the pressure while moving away from or towards the twig.

LEAVES FORMED WITH TWO BRUSHSTROKES

Moisten the bristles with light tone and scrape out excess water. Dip the tip of the brush in medium dark tone. Hold the brush in either an oblique or an upright position to form a lobed leaf. Make two oval strokes to form a pair of lobes, side by side. Add the vein along the thread of space which the two oval strokes have formed.

Holding the brush in an oblique position gives you a different effect to an upright position. Also, if you place the tip of the oblique brush at the apex of the leaf, and paint towards the leaf base, the resulting effect will differ from one created if you

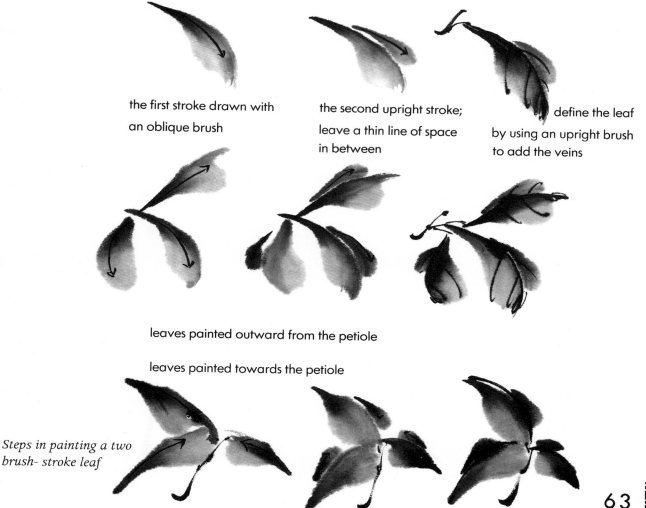

the first stroke drawn with an oblique brush

the second upright stroke; leave a thin line of space in between

define the leaf by using an upright brush to add the veins

leaves painted outward from the petiole

leaves painted towards the petiole

Steps in painting a two brush- stroke leaf

paint it outwards from the leaf base. The movement and angle of the leaf always depend on this oblique brushstroke. For the other half of the lobed leaf, use an upright brushstroke and move it along the vein line which the oblique brush has formed.

LEAVES FORMED WITH SEVERAL BRUSHSTROKES

Lotus, banana and palm leaves fall into this category. These leaves are painted with several brushstrokes of different ink tone. Use a no. 1 brush wet-loaded with a three-colour-tone. Hold the brush in an oblique position and, with a free movement of the entire arm, paint the leaf with very broad, slanting strokes. More layers of ink can be added if necessary, once the

Leaves formed with several brushstrokes

first coat has dried. The dark veins are painted in, with the tip of the no. 3 brush, when the final coat of ink on the leaf is nearly dry. Except for the lotus leaf, the main vein should be outlined first.

As the rice paper is fragile, it is necessary to wait for each stroke to dry before you begin applying the next tone over it.

NEEDLE-LIKE LEAVES

The pine leaf is the best example. Use a no. 5 brush dry-loaded in light or dark ink tone. Hold the brush in an upright position and draw the needles with the tip of the brush. Paint about ten needles in a group, starting at the pointed tips and meeting at the bottom. Paint each needle first

with the dry brush, and then apply a wet brush stroke over it to give it a soft effect.

Define the leaves later by adding the veins in black ink with the tip of an upright no. 5 brush. For new, green leaves, add the veins before the leaf blade is completely dry. A leaf's under-surface is always lighter than the surface.

Needle-like leaves

Godhawk, pine and willow. The godhawk is perched high up on a tree. Its wings half spread, its keen and watchful eye fixed on some unwary prey, it is the very personification of intensity and vigour

FLOWERS

A flower painting includes the flowers, leaves and stems. Chinese artists try to make their paintings of flowers and plants as alive as possible, using the movement of each line and an area of pure colour in each line or wash. Before you take a brush to paint, you should first observe the form of the flower, and then the position of the flower in relation to any main branches and other flowers, and finally, its colours. In Chinese painting, each flower has its symbolic meaning. Flowers and fruit-blossoms are often used to symbolize the twelve months of the year as well as the four seasons. Also, a particular flower is almost invariably drawn with a particular bird – for instance, the peony with the bulbul bird, peach blossom with the swallow, and the pine-tree with the crane.

To paint a flower piece, it is usual to do the flowers and leaves first, and then the stems. Add the veins of the leaves and dot the flower buds later. However, in certain plants, such as the Chinese orchid, lotus and the day-lily, the leaves dominate the other parts. For these plants you may do the elegant leaves and the stems first and then the flowers. To paint shrubs, such as the plum-blossom and peach-blossom, paint the branches and shoots first and then the flowers and leaves.

MOWTAN PEONY

This is the most popular flower in Chinese art, seen on silk scrolls, woodblocks and ceramics. The peony was an exceedingly popular flower among artists of the Sung Dynasty. It is

Steps in the painting of mowtan peony blossom and bud

OVERLEAF *Mowtan peony. A flower of wealth and rank*

considered by the Chinese to be the king of the flowers and a symbol of spring.

Mowtan peony is a shrub. It has biternate, large leaves, which are smooth and alternately arranged on the stems. The flowers are large and regular, with frilled petals, and come in various colours: white, cream, light to dark pink, red, crimson, blue and purple, or a combination of these. The mowtan peony has five rounded sepals and stigma surrounded by many stamens.

A mowtan peony can be painted in contour or contemporary style. For contour style, begin from the centre and then add more and more petals. For contemporary style, use a no. 2 brush moist-loaded in three-colour-tone. Hold the brush upright, and with the tip pointing towards the centre, apply pressure on the bristles and form a petal. Apply a few upright brushstrokes towards the centre. The effect is to make the flower appear alive. To complete the flower, using a no. 6 brush, add dots of yellow-white for the anthers. Use a no. 5 brush dry-loaded, and draw in the fine white filaments using upright brushstrokes.

Peony leaves are painted by using the two-brushstroke method. Use a no. 1 brush wet-loaded in three-tones, and glide the brush gently over the paper

67

Mowtan peony in ink monochrome

in a steady, even movement. Paint the veins by using a no. 5 brush dry-loaded in dark ink before the leaves are dry. The branches should look sturdy. Apply a dark brown tone with a no. 2 brush, dry-loaded, using upright brushstrokes. For the shoots, use a no. 4 brush, dry-loaded in greenish brown, and apply with upright push strokes.

a, b   *Steps in the painting of a rose*

c   *Examples of how the forms vary with different strokes*

ROSE

If the mowtan peony is the King of Flowers in China, then the rose is the Queen of Flowers in the Western world. This is the flower of love and affection, and a symbol of feminine beauty, with its fragrant, large, brilliant bloom and dazzling colour.

The rose is best painted in contemporary style. Paint the flower first followed by the buds, leaves and stems. For the flower, use a no. 2 brush moist-loaded with three-tones. Hold the brush in an upright position and paint the centre first. The rest of the petals may be applied with upright brushstrokes, oblique brushstrokes, oval strokes and circular strokes. These movements of the brush depend on the shape of the flower. Use the same brush, and same tone, to paint the bud with two oval strokes. Using a no. 5 brush dry-loaded in medium tone, paint the sepals with quick and confident upright brushstrokes.

The leaves are in clusters of five. Use a no. 2 brush moist-

upright stroke

circular stroke

oblique stroke

oval stroke

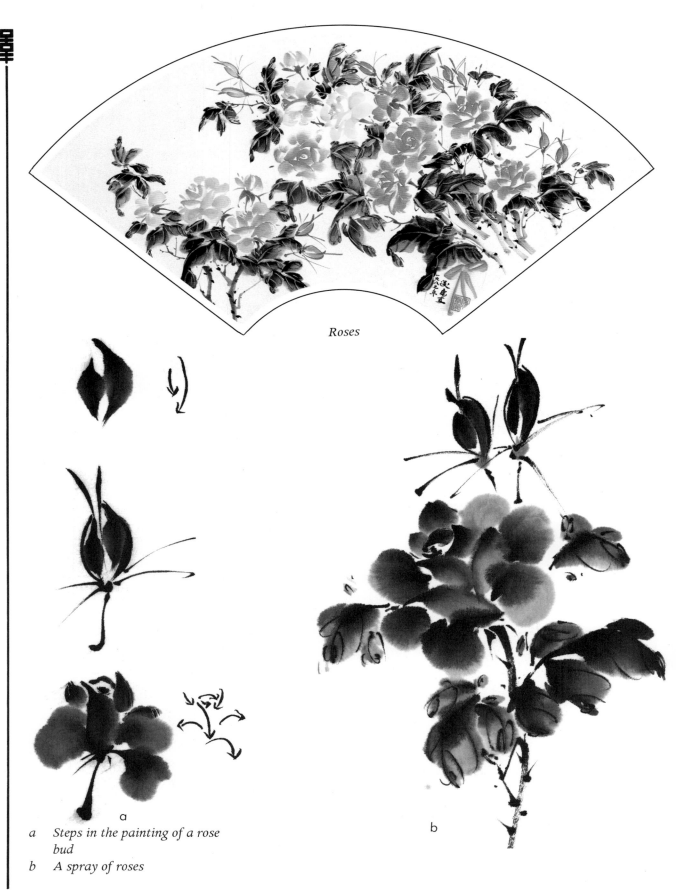

Roses

a

a   *Steps in the painting of a rose
     bud*
b   *A spray of roses*

b

loaded with a three-colour-tone, paint the leaf using the two-brushstroke method. For the stems, use either a no. 2 or a 3 brush dry-loaded in two-tones, applying the colour with upright brushstrokes. With the tip of a no. 5 brush dry-loaded in dark ink, paint the thorns.

NARCISSUS

Narcissus is a pretty, delicate blossom of early spring. It has a very special place in the history of Chinese painting. When the Chinese celebrate their New Year, one of their favourite flowers is narcissus. Its serenity and purity, and its delicate fragrance, add to the spring atmosphere.

This flower is easily painted in contour style. The slender, long, emerald-green leaves add life and movement to the flower. The large white flowers with golden coronas, and the silvery-white roots, make for a cool colour scheme.

To paint the narcissus, it is very important to work out the whole composition before you start. Use a no. 5 brush dry-loaded in light ink tone and upright brushstrokes; outline the leaves and then the flowers, bulbs and roots. Reinforce the outlines with thin and darker tone.

To apply the colour, use a no. 2 brush moist-loaded with three tones of colour. Point the tip of the brush towards the centre and press the brush gently on each petal. Use orange-red for the coronas and dot the stamens with yellow-white.

Then, using a no. 1 brush moist-loaded in two-tones or three-tones, paint the leaf with one long upright or oblique

Narcissus. The narcissus is admired for its purity of form and its flowing line

OVERLEAF *Narcissus — corona, bud, flower, leaves and bulb in contour style*

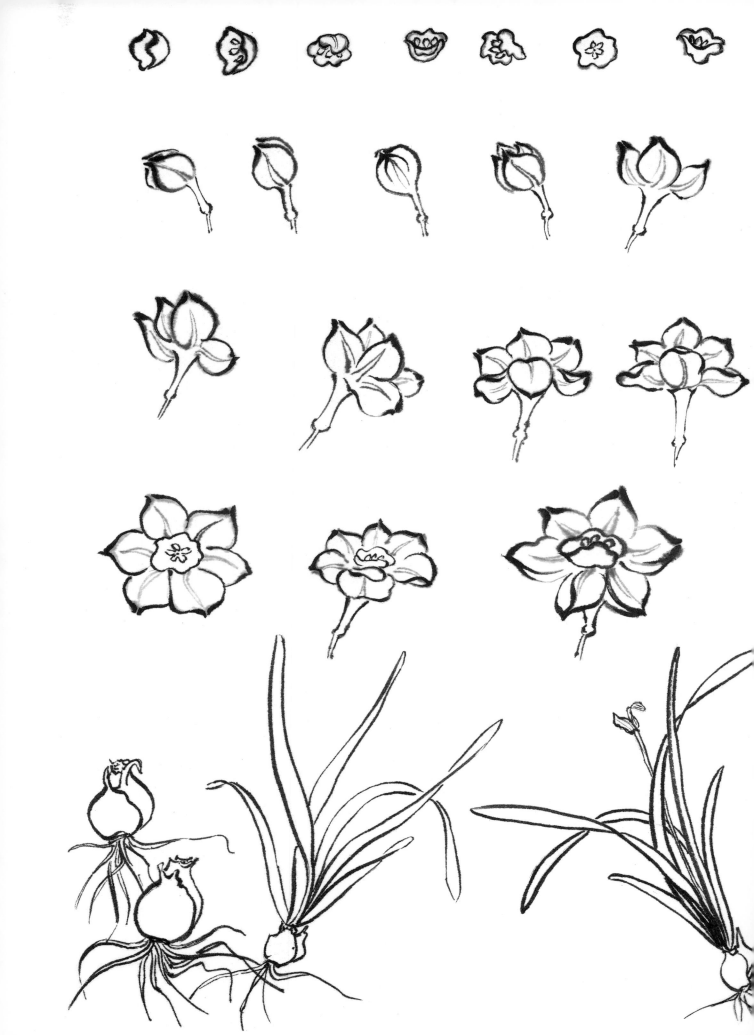

brushstroke. Add in the slim vein before the brushstroke is dry. To paint the bulb, use a no. 2 brush dry-loaded in dusty-brown and dip the tip of the brush in dark ink. Hold the brush in an upright position and with the tip pointing towards the section of the root, gently press the brush to form wash scales on the bulb. Dryer brushstrokes may be applied to emphasize the dry scales.

Camellia and bird. A joyful bird drinks in the beauty of spring. A painting to greet the new year

CAMELLIA (TEA FLOWER)

During the Ming Dynasty, the camellia was a popular motif on silk scrolls, in carved and inlaid lacquer and in porcelain.

Camellia blooms during the Chinese New Year. It is a symbol of prosperity and long life. An evergreen shrub, its leaves have a leathery texture and are either smooth-edged or toothed. It has five regular petals, with five to seven sepals. The flower petals are normally fused into a single unit and may even be attached to

the outer stamens, so that the entire flower falls in one piece, leaving only the large ovary and pistils attached to a short stem.

Camellia can be painted in contour or contemporary style. For contour style, use a no. 5 brush dry-loaded in dark ink tone. Hold the brush in an upright position and outline the flowers, buds, leaves and stems. In contemporary style, each petal is painted with one circular stroke or two oval strokes. Use a no. 2 brush moist-loaded in a three-colour-tone (yellow, vermilion and red). Fill the centre of

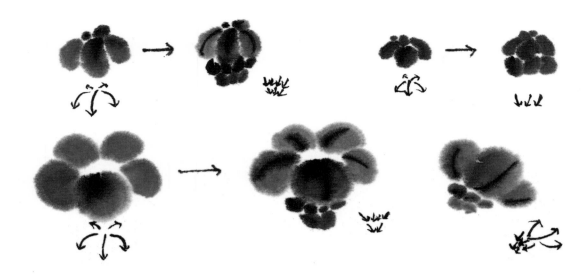

Camellia flower and bud in contemporary style

A spray of camellia in contemporary style

each flower with malachite green and paint the filaments with a no. 5 brush dry-loaded in white and yellow.

Use a no. 2 brush moist-loaded in a three-colour-tone, paint the leaf using the two brushstrokes method. Add in the vein before the brushstroke is almost dry.

With a no. 2 or no. 3 brush, medium-loaded in dark brown or dark blue, paint the branches using upright push strokes.

*Camellia leaves, flower and bud in
contour style*

LOTUS

The lotus is a symbol of purity and perfection. It grows out of the mud, into a blossom of breathtaking beauty. Its large blossoms and round tea-tray-shaped leaves are a fascinating subject for many artists. It appears in stylized form in paintings, in embroidery, on carpets and as ceramic decorations.

The lotus leaf is one of the biggest leaves of all flowering plants. It is usually borne well above the water. The pale pink, creamy-white or pale yellow flowers rise from the water in regal beauty to a height of one-and-a-half to two metres (five to seven feet). It has four sepals, many petals, and numerous golden stamens surrounding a

large poppyhead-like seed pod, which contains edible seeds. This seed pod is left exposed at the top of the stalk after the petals have fallen.

A separate, long tubular stalk supports each showy flower and each large leaf. It is very important to plan out the whole composition before you start, to ensure that you leave enough spaces for crossing or overlapping leaves and stalks.

a Contour style

All the outlinings are first done in light ink with the tip of a no. 5 brush, dry-loaded and held in an upright position. The outlines are then reinforced with a darker tone, very finely applied.

To paint a lotus flower, do the

Camellia and wax plums. Delicate flowering blossoms in harmony with the winter frost. A symbol of hope and endurance

pod head first by outlining the seed pod and the tiny circular seeds. Then outline the petals. Two or three strokes are used for each petal. Use a little pressure at the apex of the petal and draw the line towards the centre. The under-surface of the petal is finely veined with wavy lines and straight lines. Load the brush in light tone and draw in vein lines, alternating wavy line with straight line. Finally, draw in the stamens, and then dot the anthers in dark ink.

The leaves can be shown in

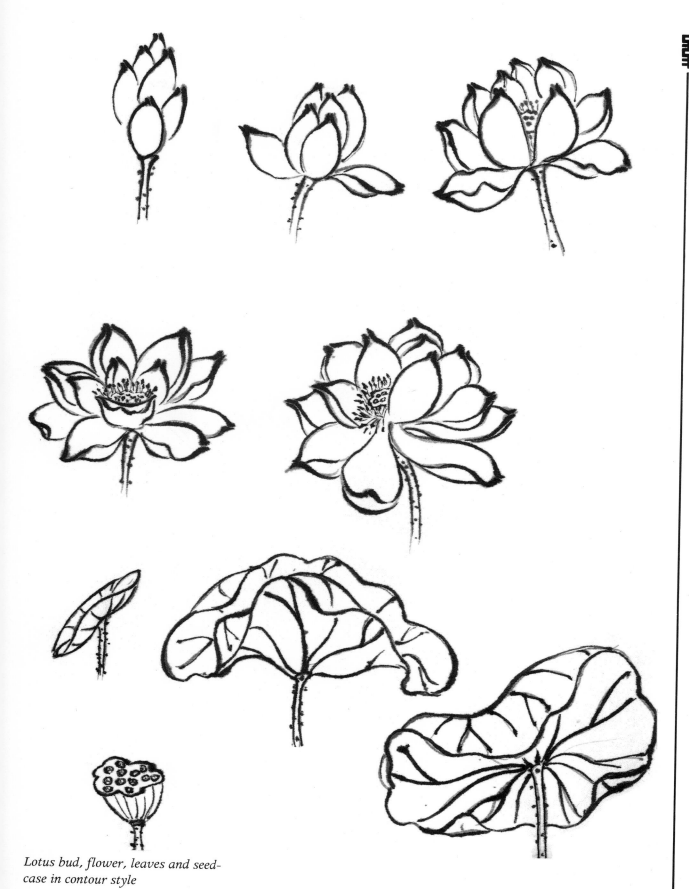

Lotus bud, flower, leaves and seed-case in contour style

various stages of growth, as they unfold from a slightly folded position, and open out to large round tea-tray-like leaves. Use a no. 4 brush, dry-loaded in medium tone, to draw the veins radiating from the centre to the leaf edge. Alternate the vein lines, a straight-vein line with a forked-vein line.

The stalks are always added last. With a no. 5 brush dry-loaded in medium tone, draw two long, smooth lines. Dot the lines and the space in between to produce a prickly stalk. Each flower, leaf and bud has its own individual stalk. The leaf stalks are darker than the flower stalks.

If you do the contour style in colour, use a technique similar to the one described for the narcissus, the only exception being that each vein of the leaf consists of two fine lines drawn close together. Leave the space between these lines unpainted.

b Contemporary style

The flowers may differ in colour – vermilion red, white or creamy-white. Note that the outer face of the petal is darker than the inner face. To paint the petal, use a no. 1 or 2 brush, wet-loaded in three tones. Place the brush at the edge of the petal and paint inwards towards the flower base. The petal can be painted in two brushstrokes. Use either two upright brushstrokes or two oblique brushstrokes. Use a no. 5 brush, dry-loaded in light tone, to draw in the veins on the underside of each petal. Do this while the petal is still wet. Then use a no. 5 brush, dry-loaded in light tone, to draw the yellow fine lines of the filaments, and add white dots for the anthers.

To paint a leaf, first observe its poise. Use a no. 4 brush, dry-

ABOVE *Lotus and kingfisher. Chou Tzu called the lotus 'superior among flowers', and so it symbolizes the noble character of a gentleman scholar*

RIGHT *Lotus in contour and contemporary styles (method 1)*

loaded in dark tone, to paint a few lines, each radiating from the centre to suggest the main veins of the leaf. Now use a no. 1 brush, wet-loaded in three-tones. Place the tip of the brush towards the centre. Hold brush obliquely and with a free movement of the entire arm, make a broad sweeping stroke. Use the main vein as your guide-line, and vary the tones of your brushstrokes, some darker than the others. The top surface of the lotus leaf is darker than the underside. Moist brushstrokes suggest new, growing leaves, and dry brushstrokes, withered leaves.

To paint the small, divided leaf, use a no. 2 brush wet-loaded in darker tone, and apply two upright strokes. Add the veins before the brushstrokes are dry.

For the long stalk, again use a no. 2 brush, this time dry-loaded in light green (flower stalk) or dark green (leaf stalk). Dip the tip of the brush in dark ink. Hold the brush in an upright position, and from the base of each leaf, flower or bud, apply one long, smooth downward stroke. Finally, use a no. 4 brush dry-loaded in dark ink to stipple the stalk with black dots.

To paint the pods, use a no. 2 brush wet-loaded in light ink, and apply it with a broad, flowing, upright stroke. Wash with brownish-green. Apply dots of dark green for the seeds. Each dot is rimmed in a lighter tone of the same colour.

LEFT *Lotus in contour and contemporary styles (methods 2 and 3)*

RIGHT *Steps in the painting of the lotus leaf (contemporary method)*

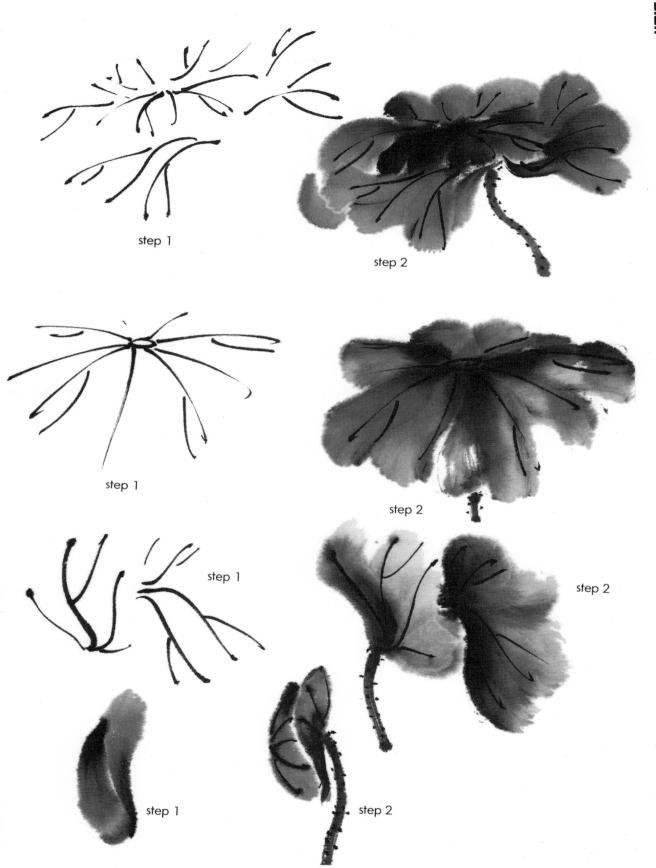

step 1

step 2

step 1

step 2

step 1

step 1

step 2

step 1

step 2

WISTERIA

A beautiful deciduous, twining climber, the wisteria has long flower clusters of mauve or purple, pea-shaped blooms that appear in spring. Chinese artists like to paint the swallow, fish or

Wisteria leaves, stem and flower in contour and contemporary styles

duckling with this flower. With flowers hanging on twining stems, and twigs with young leaves dangling in the air, the whole picture suggests a gentle breeze stirring in the thick foliage of the plant.

The wisteria petals are painted with a no. 2 brush, moist-loaded in two or three tones of colour. Hold the brush upright with the

tip pointing towards the stem. Add pressure and rotate the brush handle to the left, and then shift the brush to the right. This time rotate the brush handle between the fingers, in a clockwise direction. In this way, two semi-circled petals are formed. These two petals should be loosely attached. Do not allow the petals to overlap. Fill the space in between with two yellow dots. Then paint two deep purple blobs with a no. 3 brush, dry-loaded, using short curved strokes. The flower buds are done in deep purple using short, curved strokes.

To paint the drooping leaves, first paint a faint twig using a no. 5 brush, dry-loaded in dark brown. Then, using a no. 2 brush, moist-loaded in two or three tones of colour, paint the leaf starting from the tip, using the one brushstroke method. Do one side first, then reload the colour-tone and do the other side.

The twining stems are painted with a no. 3 or no. 5 brush dry-loaded in dark brown. Hold the brush in an upright position, and paint the twining stems using dragging strokes.

To paint the wisteria in contour style, use a no. 5 brush dry-loaded in medium ink-tone, and outline the twining stems and twigs. Reinforce the outline with a thin line in dark tone.

HYDRANGEA

Hydrangea consists of an inflorescence of small flowers, each flower comprising four regular petals with the stamen in the centre. The flower is large and pink, blue-white or lavender in colour. It makes a very fine and colourful display throughout summer and early autumn. It has four sepals and alternate, serrated leaves.

This flower is a pleasure to paint in contemporary style. Just press your brush four times to form each flower. Before you realize it, you have formed a large flower head.

To paint the flower, use a no. 2 brush, medium-loaded in three tones of colour, and upright brushstrokes. Gently press four times for each flower. The flowers should cluster together in a natural way; the final shape should be relatively round but not circular. Add a dot to the centre of each flower.

Paint the leaves with a no. 1 brush by using the two-brush-stroke method. Add veins before they are dry. Use a firm and positive upright brushstroke to paint the stem.

Hydrangea flowers, leaves and buds in contour and contemporary styles

TOP RIGHT *Hydrangea, or 'xiuqui-hua', to celebrate a wedding: 'xiuqui' is a ball made of strips of silk. During a traditional wedding ceremony, the bride and groom each hold one end of the 'xiuqui', symbolizing unity*

BOTTOM RIGHT *A spray of hydrangea in ink monochrome*

BIRDS

In traditional Chinese flower and blossom painting, a bird often makes a good companion to the flowers, not only because it gives life and movement to the picture, but also because it refers symbolically to character traits. A crane and bulbul bird, for instance, suggest longevity, a pair of mandarin ducks represents happy marriage, and the eagle signifies boldness and keen vision.

Before painting a bird, the anatomy, life and nature of the bird should be considered. Observe how the bird flies, sings, pecks and eats. A flying bird stretches its wings and tail, opens its eyes and closes its claws. A resting bird has its claws holding fast on to the tree and its eyeballs turned to one side. When a bird sings, its mouth is open and its tongue visible. A bird looking for food will stoop and peck at something.

It may seem difficult to learn to paint a bird, the more so because painting it directly on the rice paper means you cannot afford to make any stroke mistake. Also, you cannot outline the bird in pencil on the rice paper. It is fairly easy to overcome this problem, however. First, draw a bird from a basic egg shape. Observe and study the bird's natural habitat to get an idea of its different postures and movements. Then, draw the bird on rice paper with a drawing pencil. After this, put the drawing under your original painting paper for tracing. This

RIGHT *Painting a bird in different postures*

FAR RIGHT *Snowy owl and pine tree.*

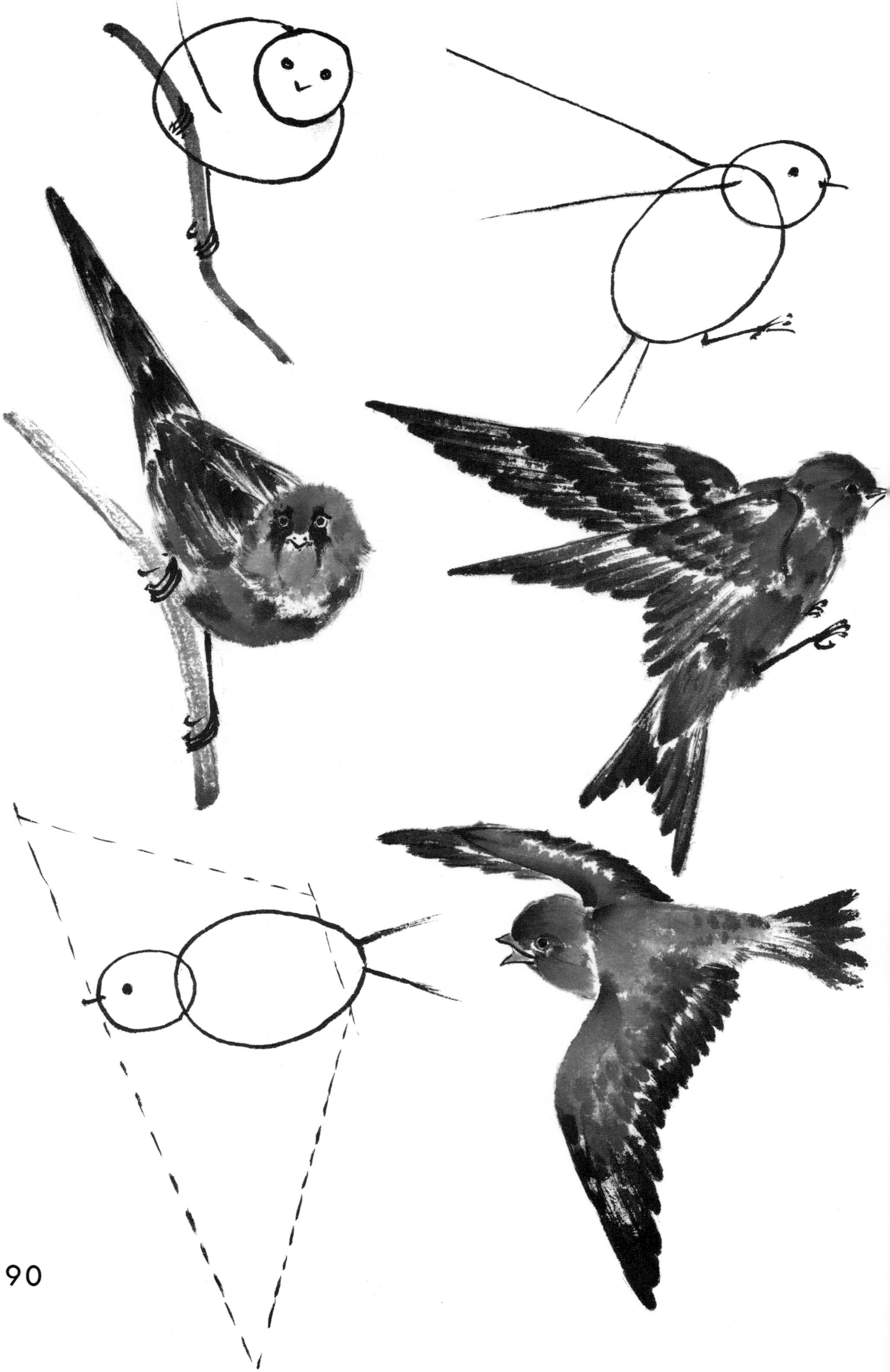

Steps in the painting of birds

ABOVE *Brushstrokes used for various parts of a bird*

head

neck

back

front

breast

back

brush tip pointing towards the base of the beak, gently press the brush down, and slightly swing the brush to one side, thus allowing the upper bristles of the brush to make contact with the surface of the paper. One important point to note is that the brushstroke should not overlay the eye.

The neck

Use a no. 2 brush moist-loaded in light tone. Hold the brush upright and with the brush tip pointing towards the beak, press down. You may use the no. 4 or no. 5 brush to define the hairs.

Back and breast

Use a no. 2 brush moist-loaded in medium tone. Make two oblique strokes to form the back and breast of the bird.

Wing and tail

This is an important part in the art of painting birds, and requires a confident use of the brushstroke technique. Use a no. 2 brush dry-loaded in a darker tone, and paint the wing with an upright brushstroke, with the brush tip touching the paper. Drag it towards the bird's body. Stroke by stroke, paint the feathers starting from those at the front row to the outer longer feathers.

To paint the tail, make dragging movements outward with the brush tip, starting from the end of the body. This method is used for the crane. However, for the long-tailed tit and blue-tit, the brush tip is dragged towards the body (see illustration).

Belly and thigh

Use a no. 2 brush wet-loaded in a light tone. Make upright brushstrokes.

helps you concentrate on the actual brushstrokes as you do not have to draw the bird. You may skip this method once you have mastered the art of the brushstrokes. The following

guidelines are for a painting in contemporary style.

The beak

Using a small no. 5 brush, dry-loaded in dark tone, apply an upright brushstroke.

The eyes

Place a no. 5 brush, dry-loaded in dark tone, near to the roof of the bill and paint the pupil of the eye. Draw the eyelid, if needed.

Forehead

Use a no. 2 brush wet-loaded with three tones of colour. Hold the brush upright, and with the

Using a no. 4 or 5 brush, dry-loaded in darker tones, apply upright brushstrokes.

Finally, use a no. 6 blunt brush to draw the fine hairs. Or, hold a no. 2 brush, dry-loaded, in an upright position, and pressing the brush bristles between the thumb and the first finger, define the hairs.

Brushstrokes used for painting the wings and the tail

一九八八年 受廣 畫

Pine tree and blue-tits. A con-
gratulatory painting to the happy
couple on their wedding day, and a
wish for three kinds of abundance:
longevity (pine); good fortune and
male offspring (nuts); and peace
and harmony (a pair of birds)

Brushstrokes used for painting a butterfly and dragonfly

INSECTS

There are many kinds of insects, and the Chinese painter loves to paint these small creatures. They will enliven a flower-composition as they gather round the flowers, collecting their fragrance, or climbing along the stems and alighting on the leaves. Their presence can also be a subtle hint of the advent of spring, summer or autumn.

Insects are usually placed in flower paintings as an ornamental addition. When painting insects, you should bear in mind their seasonal activities and their complicated behaviour pattern in relation to their surroundings.

Insects can be painted in either the contour style or the contemporary style. When painting insects, the usual order to follow is to paint the head first followed by the body and the wings and lastly, the legs. However, when painting an insect with big wings, for example a butterfly, do the wings first and then the other parts. Use a no. 5 brush to draw the outline and the veins in the wing. Use solid strokes for the legs. For small insects, use hair-like strokes. Use a bigger brush to do the shading and to give texture to the body and wings. Ink-wash or colour may be added later.

BUTTERFLY

The butterfly is not only a symbol of summer but is also regarded as an emblem of joy. It is a well-known insect whose membranous wings are covered with beautiful designs and are often brightly coloured. The mouthparts are in the form of a proboscis, which can be coiled up while flying. When alighting on a flower, the proboscis extends out for sucking nectar and the large wings are vertically closed.

As the butterfly is an insect with big, colourful wings, paint the wings first and then use dark ink to delineate the other parts.

The wing

Use a no. 2 brush wet-loaded in light tone. Dip the tip of the brush in dark tone. Hold the brush upright with the tip pointing towards the body, press down lightly and form a wing in

Steps in the painting of a bee, grasshopper and mantis

one simple stroke. To form the hind wing, press the brush lightly and then rotate the brush to form a circular stroke. When the wing is nearly dry, use a no. 5 brush dry-loaded in a darker tone to apply some spots or designs on the wing. Use a light tone for drawing in the veins.

The body

Use a no. 6 brush wet-loaded in light tone. Hold the upright brush at a slight angle to the paper, press down, and form a short dot for the body, and a long, curved stroke for the tail. Use a no. 5 brush, dry-loaded and dipped in dark ink, to draw

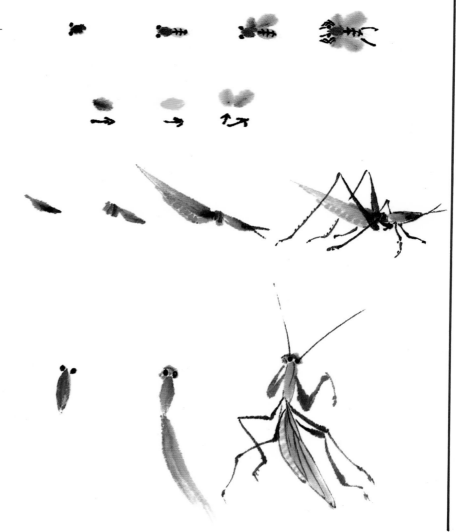

The wings

Use a no. 2 brush wet-loaded in light blue or light ink tone. Hold the brush upright and with the tip placed at the side of the body, press down to form one fine delicate wing.

Use a no. 5 brush, dry-loaded in dark tone, to paint the rest of the body, the eyes, antennae and the legs. Apply quick upright brushstrokes.

DRAGONFLY

This insect is often seen flying around trees, and near swift-flowing rivers, streams and lakes on hot summer days. It is a brightly coloured insect with two pairs of long, glass-like wings, which have a network of fine veins, large eyes, very short antennae and a long, slender tail. Its wings are held over its back when at rest. The thorax bears its slender legs and the two pairs of large membranous wings.

Hawker dragonfly

Use a no. 6 brush wet-loaded in light green or light blue. Hold the brush upright to form the large compound eyes which cover almost the entire surface of the head. Paint the body of the dragonfly in yellow-green, yellow or blue. Hold the no. 3 brush, dry-loaded, upright, and with a quick stroke form the slender abdomen and tail. While it is still moist, apply black ink to outline the body. Then use a no. 2 brush moist-loaded in light tone. Dip the tip of the brush in slightly darker tone. Hold the

the curved line on the tail. Then, using the same small brush, dry-loaded in dark tone, apply upright brushstrokes to paint the antennae, eyes, legs and fine hairs on the abdomen.

To paint the butterfly in contour style, first outline the wing and body. When dry, apply the wash. Draw in the rest using a no. 5 brush, dry-loaded in dark tone.

BEE

The bee is an insect of variable size. It has two pairs of membranous wings that have a few veins. Its body has black and yellow rings round it. At rest, the wings are folded over the back. The hard-working bee is an emblem of industry and thrift.

The head

Moisten a no. 6 brush in light ink or brownish-grey colour. Apply one slow, lightly pressed, upright brushstroke.

The body

Moisten a no. 6 brush in yellow and coat the tip of the paint brush with brown or black. Slowly press down, with upright brush, to form the body in just one stroke. While the body of the bee is still moist, use a no. 5 brush, dipped in black ink, to draw the curved lines on it.

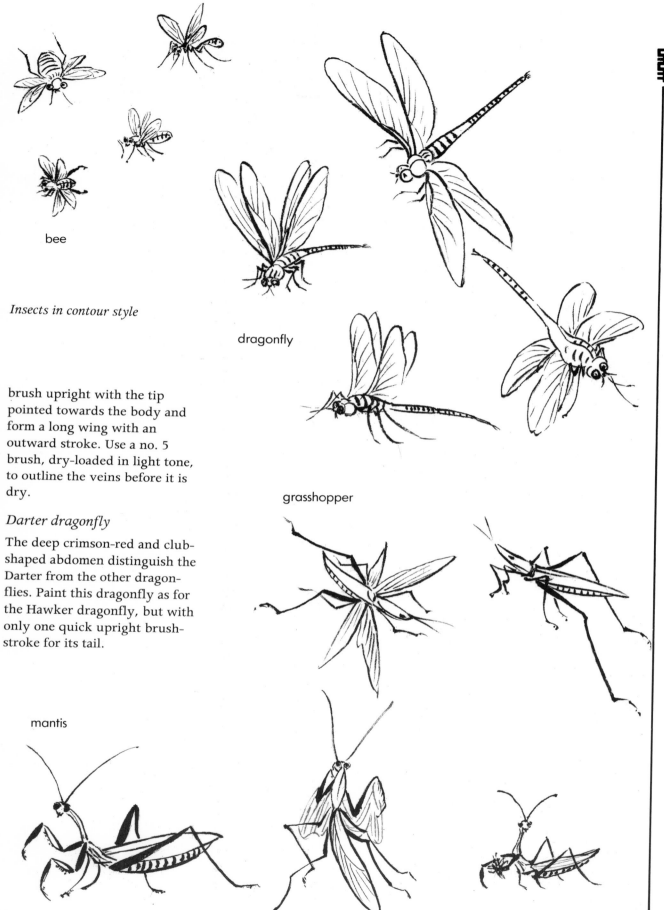

bee

Insects in contour style

dragonfly

brush upright with the tip pointed towards the body and form a long wing with an outward stroke. Use a no. 5 brush, dry-loaded in light tone, to outline the veins before it is dry.

Darter dragonfly

The deep crimson-red and club-shaped abdomen distinguish the Darter from the other dragon-flies. Paint this dragonfly as for the Hawker dragonfly, but with only one quick upright brush-stroke for its tail.

grasshopper

mantis

GRASSHOPPER

The grasshopper has typical biting mouthparts, two long antennae and well-developed wings. Although it can fly, it moves mainly by hopping on a pair of powerful hind-legs attached to the thorax. The hind wings are well-developed and are folded like a fan when at rest. It moves by prodigious leaps and flights, on hot, sunny days, mainly in August and September. In early October, it disappears.

The head

Use a no. 6 brush, medium-loaded in medium tone, to form its head, with just one upright brushstroke.

The body

To form the thorax, use a no. 6 brush dry-loaded in darker tone. Hold the brush upright and press three times. To form the abdomen, use the no. 6 brush wet-loaded in medium tone. Hold brush upright and make several, quick, slightly-curved strokes.

The wings

Use a no. 3 brush, moist-loaded in light tone. Dip the tip of the brush in slightly darker tone. Hold the brush upright with the tip pointing towards the thorax, press, and form a long wing with a quick outward stroke. Use a no. 5 brush dry-loaded in light tone to outline the veins before it is dry.

With a no. 5 brush dry-loaded in dark tone, paint the legs, eyes and antennae.

MANTIS

The mantis has a freely moving, triangular-shaped head with biting mouthparts. Its long and narrow prothorax bears a pair of raptorial legs (i.e. modified for seizing prey). The wings are well-developed, especially the hind pair. When at rest, the fore wings lie flat over the back, the larger hind wings folded.

The mantis is painted in the same way as the grasshopper.

FISH

A fish is the symbol of wealth and abundance. Owing to its reproductive powers, it is also a symbol of regeneration. In Chinese painting, the fish is always painted swimming in the water, usually among the water weeds.

When painting the fish, paint the head first, then the body and then the tail.

The head

Use a no. 5 brush dry-loaded in dark tone; paint the eye, the mouth and then the nose. Use thick charred ink to depict the eye. To complete the head, use a no. 2 brush wet-loaded in light tone. Then dip the brush tip in darker tone. Pointing the tip of the brush towards the edge of the forehead, form the forehead with one oblique drag stroke towards the gills. Use thick black ink to delineate the forehead. Use a no. 5 brush, dry-loaded in light tone, to draw the brim of the gill-cover.

Steps in the painting of a goldfish

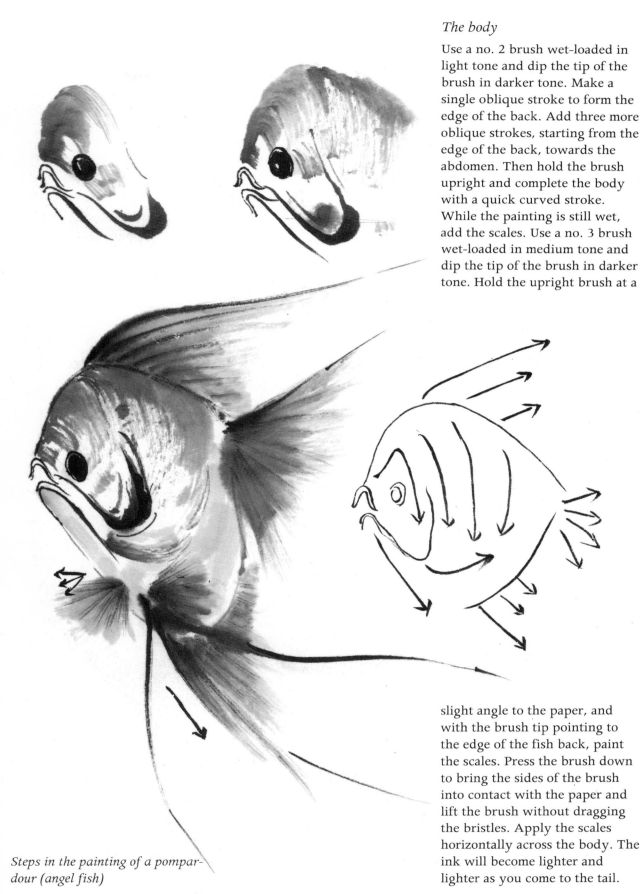

The body

Use a no. 2 brush wet-loaded in light tone and dip the tip of the brush in darker tone. Make a single oblique stroke to form the edge of the back. Add three more oblique strokes, starting from the edge of the back, towards the abdomen. Then hold the brush upright and complete the body with a quick curved stroke. While the painting is still wet, add the scales. Use a no. 3 brush wet-loaded in medium tone and dip the tip of the brush in darker tone. Hold the upright brush at a

slight angle to the paper, and with the brush tip pointing to the edge of the fish back, paint the scales. Press the brush down to bring the sides of the brush into contact with the paper and lift the brush without dragging the bristles. Apply the scales horizontally across the body. The ink will become lighter and lighter as you come to the tail.

Steps in the painting of a pompar-dour (angel fish)

The tail

Use a no. 2 brush wet-loaded in light tone, and dip the brush tip in darker tone. Hold the brush in an oblique position make a quick, firm outward stroke to form the tail.

The fins

Use a no. 2 brush wet-loaded in light tone. Press the oblique brush from the leading edge and stroke outward. The fin is done in a single oblique brushstroke.

To delineate the fins and tail, use a no. 2 brush dry-loaded in darker tone. Flatten the bristles with your thumb and first finger, and make outward brushstrokes. Do this while the painting is still wet.

A pair of goldfish. Symbolizing a happy marriage, this is a painting to congratulate the wedding couple

5

THE 'FOUR PARAGONS'

Cranes and plum blossom. Plum blossom is one of the four paragons or noble plants, which are so-called because they represent the highest Chinese virtues. The plum blossom symbolizes fortitude and venerable old age; the orchid, piety; the bamboo, loyalty and courage in adversity; and the chrysanthemum, the unworldly scholar and recluse

PLUM BLOSSOM

Plum blossom is a symbol of hope and longevity. Chinese artists never tire of the poetry of the pale blossoms springing from the gnarled bare black boughs. To paint the plum blossom, start with the bough, then move on to the shoot, moss, flower, stamen and lastly the sepals.

CONTEMPORARY STYLE

Bough

Moisten the large no. 2 brush in clear water. Then load the brush in light tone. Gently scrape the top of the bristles on the edge of the plate so that this upper section is only slightly loaded. Roll the tip of the brush in a darker tone. Allow a second for the dark tone to rise into the bristles. The dark tone becomes increasingly diluted towards the top of the bristles. Again, dip the tip of the brush in a darker tone. Hold the brush obliquely, and, starting from the thickest part of the bough and moving towards the thinnest part, gently pull the brush along in a somewhat jagged path. The result is an irregular, angular-looking line. As you move the brush along, alternate between pressing down and lightly dragging it to create moist and dry areas. This expresses the characteristic roughness of the bough and gives it an aged appearance.

NOTE. When the petals are painted in contemporary style, the boughs must also be painted in contemporary style.

Shoots

Use a no. 3 brush to draw the shoots jutting out from the boughs. Hold the brush upright and paint in the direction of

Plum blossom in contour style

growth, moving from one junction to another. First, press the brush down at one junction. Release the pressure and then glide the tip smoothly to the next junction. The tone of the shoots may vary from medium to light, becoming lighter as it reaches upward or outward. Re-ink when necessary. Vary the lengths of the shoots and their thicknesses, as well as their position. The shoots often have thin, straight spurs issuing from them and darting off in all directions.

As you move your brush along to form the boughs, shoots and spurs, you must visualize the position of each blossom, so that spaces can be left in between for them. They may overlap and hide parts of the boughs, shoots or spurs. Allow your shoots to cross one another in an interest-

a   Plum blossom in various positions in contemporary style
b   Centre of flower stamen
c   Sepals

ing pattern. The shoots are always painted in contemporary style to maintain the strength of a single line.

Moss

To help delineate the boughs and shoots and also to create an impression of natural incrustations, add some 'moss' dots. Use a no. 2 or 3 brush, moist-loaded in medium tone. Dip the brush in dark ink. With the tip of the brush, dabble here and there along the boughs and shoots. For colour compositions, use yellow-green or blue-green.

Flowers

A plum blossom has five rounded petals. However, it can be represented by fewer petals, even one. Paint the blossoms in different positions, some facing the viewer, some fully turned away. Also paint the blossoms in different aspects, ranging from tightly closed buds to fully opened blossoms. The differences can be made apparent by

the shape and position of each petal, as well as the placement of the stamens and sepals.

Plum blossoms may be painted in black-and-white or in colour, white-pink or yellow-white. First moisten the bristles in a medium tone. Then dip the tip of the brush in a darker tone. Hold the brush in a slightly oblique position. Place the tip of the brush at the centre and then slowly add pressure as you paint outwards to form a round petal. The more petals or buds that are formed, the lighter the ink or colour tone becomes. Judge for yourself when to re-ink or re-colour the brush. Remember, the undersides of petals are lighter in colour.

Stamen

Inside the flower, there is a collection of dotted filaments surrounding a single pistil. These filaments are irregular in length and spacing. Use a darker tone to contrast with the petals. With the tip of a no. 5 brush, dipped in dark ink, draw in the dotted filaments. For colour compositions, use dark blue for the lines, and white or pale yellow for the dots.

Sepals

The stamen and sepals are added after the petals and buds are dry. Make sure the sepals reach from the shoot to the flower or bud. Use a no. 4 brush, dipped in dark ink. For colour compositions, use dark blue or dark green.

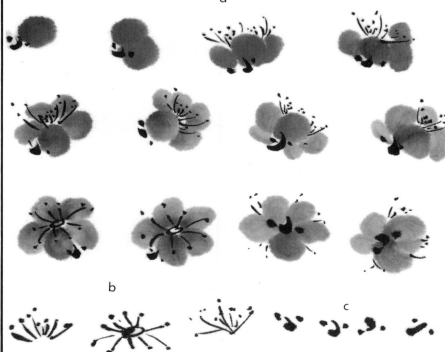

a

b

c

RIGHT *Bamboo and plum blossom. More new year greetings. The bamboo brings tidings of peace, and plum blossom represents good fortune*

CONTOUR STYLE

Boughs

Use a no. 5 brush dry-loaded in a light tone. With upright brush-strokes and using only the tip of the brush, outline the boughs. Then fill in the space in between with washes of light or medium tone. After the first wash has dried, apply a darker wash to produce form and texture. Add dark ink to accentuate the contours. For colour compositions, mix blue with brown, or with ink; or use blue and yellow.

LEFT *Plum blossom (contemporary style)*
BELOW *Hui orchid in contour style*

Flowers

Use a no. 5 brush dry-loaded in light tone, and with the tip of the brush outline the buds and petals. After these outlines are dry, go over them with a thinner line in a darker tone to emphasize the shape and form of each bud and petal. For colour compositions, use white-pink or white-yellow.

CHINESE ORCHID

The orchid is a favourite subject for ink artists because of its delicate curving lines and simplicity of form. There are two species of wild orchid. The spring orchid, called 'lan', has only one flower or bud on each main stem. The leaves grow in tufts of not more than seven blades. The summer orchid, 'hui', has several flowers or buds on one main stem and has not more than eleven blades of delicately curving leaves.

Paint the orchid when you are in a tranquil mood. When you are calm and relaxed, you are best able to identify yourself with the orchid plant, the leaves swaying and the buds opening joyfully in the breeze. In painting the orchid, first paint the leaves, then the main stem and sheath, followed by the bud or flower, the heart of the flower, and lastly the stalks.

Lan orchid in contemporary style

Leaves

The leaf-blades should be painted according to the order shown in the illustrations. If you do not follow the proper order, you may find that instead of orchid leaves, you have painted a clump of grass.

1 Paint the first blade in a long arc.
2 The second stroke crosses the first stroke forming a 'phoenix-eye' with the first stroke.
3 The third stroke goes through the 'phoenix-eye' cutting it into two halves.
4 The fourth stroke cuts across the third stroke.
5 The fifth stroke crosses over the first blade, and if it is longer, cuts across the second blade as well.
6 The sixth stroke is very short, at the base of the plant.

Long leaf-blades

Use a no. 2 brush moist-loaded in medium and dark ink tone. Dip the tip of the brush in the darker tone. With an upright brush-stroke, starting from the base of the plant, make one continuous upward stroke. Gradually add pressure to broaden the leaf-blade at mid-length, and then decrease the pressure by gradually lifting the brush when approaching the tip. The brush movement should flow smoothly in an arc-shape to the left or to the right. Gently rotate the brush between the fingers if you wish to paint a leaf turning in a new direction.

Short leaf-blades

The leaves at the base of the orchid plant are shorter. They should be straight and stiff. Use a

no. 2 brush moist-loaded in darker tone. Hold the brush upright and stroke upwards from the roots. Add pressure at the beginning to give a broader base, and then gradually decrease the pressure, lifting off the brush near the tip.

Leaf blades should be painted according to the order shown.
TOP *leaf blades curved to the left*
BELOW *leaf blades curved to the right*

THE FOUR PARAGONS

109

Paint the leaves in the background in a lighter tone. In general all the leaves should be painted in a darker tone than the flower. For colour compositions, use indigo, yellow and umber.

Stem

The stem is erect and strong, but supple and pliable. You can paint the stem straight, or leaning slightly to the left or right. Use a no. 5 brush moist-loaded in medium tone. With the tip of the upright brush make one graceful stroke from the top of the plant towards the base.

The spring orchid, 'lan', has a shorter main stem. It can be painted in one bold stroke. The summer orchid, 'hui', has a longer main stem. Allow a short pause in the middle of your brushstroke movement at the point where you wish to indicate a slight change in direction. For colour compositions, use a light, yellowish-green. After it is dry, apply a colour-wash in umber.

Sheath

The sheath is the short and wide wrapping at the base of the stem. Use a no. 3 brush moist-loaded in medium tone. Make one upright brushstroke from the tip of the sheath to the base on one side of the stem. Make another similar brushstroke on the other side. For colour compositions, load the brush with the three colours – indigo, yellow and umber.

Bud

A bud can be painted in one, two or three brushstrokes. Use a no. 2 or 3 brush, moist-loaded in medium tone. Apply the ink in one upright brushstroke from the tip of the bud to the base. The second petal should be very slender; again, apply the ink

Orchid and bees. The orchid buds open joyfully and the leaves appear to flutter. The orchid's attraction lies in its perfection and simplicity of form

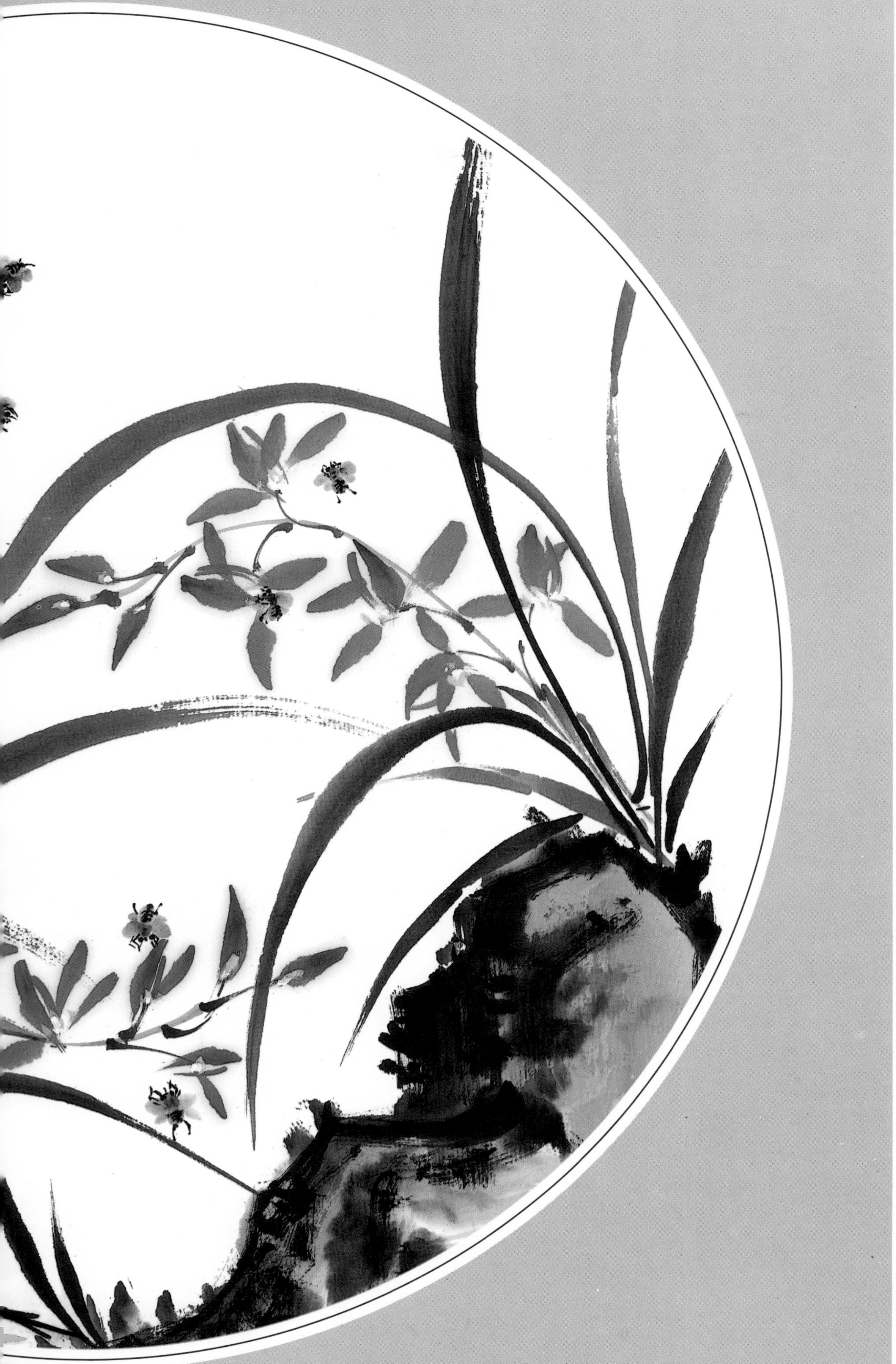

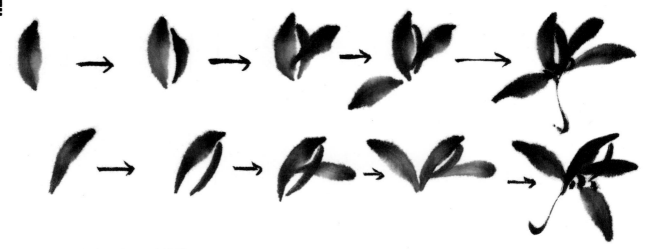

*Steps in painting the orchid flower
in contemporary style*

from the tip to the base. For a
bud that is partially opening,
add a third petal to the side of
the two-petalled bud.

Flower

The orchid blossom has five
petals. Using a no. 2 or 3 brush,
moist-loaded in two or three
tones, make one quick brushstroke for each petal, by painting
from the tip of the petal inward,
towards the flower base. Apply
slight pressure for a broadening
effect, and allow the brush to
glide without pressure at the tip.

The orchid blossoms should be
painted in various positions;
some partially turned, or fully
turned, with half-hidden hearts,
and some presenting an open
face with an exposed heart. For
colour compositions, use red; or
pink and white; or purple and
yellow; or light purple and
white; or light umber, or light
green and white.

Dotting the heart

Use a no. 4 brush dry-loaded
with thick black ink to dot the
centre of the flower before the
petals are dry. The black ink will

*Outlining the orchid leaves,
contour style*

slightly run into the lighter tone of the petal. This produces a dewy effect.

For a slightly opened flower, press one dot with the tip of the brush. For a half-opened blossom, press a dot at the centre and a larger dot extending outward. For a fully opened blossom, press three dots.

For colour compositions, use a darker tone, or a lighter tone of the colours that you have used for flowers. The tone depends on individual preference.

Stalks

After the buds and flowers have been painted, draw in the stalks. Use a no. 5 brush, medium-loaded. Using the tip, and with an upright brushstroke, drag the brush towards the base of the flower from the main stem. For colour compositions, use light yellowish-green and colour wash with umber.

CONTOUR STYLE IN INK AND COLOUR

With the tip of a no. 5, upright brush, first outline in pale ink the leaf-blades, main stem, buds or flowers, hearts and stalks. After these outlines are dry, go over them with a thinner, darker ink line to emphasize the shape. The flowers or leaves are shown in various positions, and thus the lines may vary slightly in width.

Leaves and sheath

The main colours to use are indigo, yellow and umber, though you are not bound by any specific mix of colour. Let your experience and personal preference guide you. Use a no. 2 brush loaded with two or three tones of colour. Apply in one spontaneous stroke. Dip a no. 5

Outlining the orchid flowers and sheaths, contour style

brush in a dark tone to draw the veins. Apply a lighter tone for the underside of the leaf-blade.

Bud and flower

After the ink outlines are dry, fill the petals and hearts with white. Colour the top of the petals in red or purple. Then, with a moist clean brush, wash the colour from the top towards the base.

Apply light green over the base of the petal. Now, with a moist clean brush, wash the light green upward. After the washes are dry, use a deeper red tone to wash over the petals. Draw the veins on the petals. Dot the heart with deep red tone.

Alternatively, use any of the following colours: red; pink and white; purple and yellow; light purple and white; light umber, or light green and white. Using no. 2 brush, moist-loaded with two or three tones, fill in the spaces after the outlines have dried.

Main stem and stalks

After the outlines have dried, use a no. 2 brush, moist-loaded with light yellowish green, to fill in the spaces. Wash with umber when dry.

BAMBOO

Bamboo is the most popular plant subject for ink painting and the most appropriate, for calligraphy. Its elegant long stems and clusters of leaves constantly change pattern as they move and bend in the wind. The painting of bamboo allows the artist to attain the Chinese ideal of expressing on paper a sensitive observation of nature with vibrant feeling. A Yüan Dynasty artist wrote that he always painted the bamboo in anger. He explained that one should paint the bamboo in an excited state of mind in order to produce powerful brushstrokes, and claimed that the bristling leaves of the bamboo, sticking outward like spears, allow the expression of anger. Certainly, painting the bamboo is an exercise in virtuosity in ink brushwork.

Contemporary style

To paint the bamboo start with the stem, then move on to the joints and branches, and lastly the leaves.

Stem

Bear in mind that

- it is the slender hollow stem that allows the bamboo to bend and spring back under a strong wind
- the sections of a bamboo stem increase in length as the plant grows taller. Therefore those sections that are nearest the ground and those at the top of the stem are shortest
- a bamboo stem may bend in any direction. It bends at the joints. The sections between the joints do not bend

ABOVE *Bamboo in contemporary style* RIGHT *Bamboo in contour style*

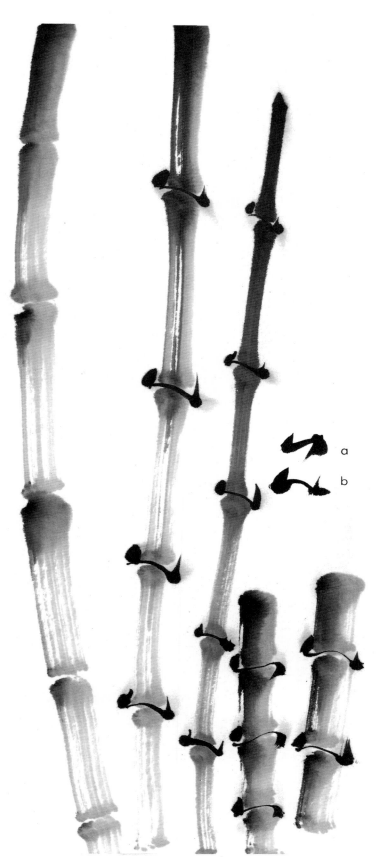

Moisten a no. 2 or 3 brush in clear water. Load the brush with a light ink tone. Tap out excess moisture. Dip the tip in a darker ink tone. Hold the brush upright with the brush tip pointing towards the left of your paper. Start from the top of the paper. Apply pressure on the bristles, and quickly drag the brush downward, in one upright brushstroke, to stop at the first joint. Press your brush down slightly at the joint before lifting it from the paper. Leave a narrow space for the joint and then paint the next section in the same manner. Repeat this until you have completed your stem.

The edges of the stem should be distinct, so reload your brush whenever necessary. The width of your stem depends on the amount of bristles which are allowed to come into contact with the paper. For dry, old broken stems, use a dry-loaded brush. If there are two stems standing side by side, paint one stem darker than the other. If there are three or more stems, paint the stems in the foreground in darker tones.

Joints

After painting the stem, paint the joints. The joints should be painted slightly curved upward at each end, to give a rounded form to the stem. Use a no. 4 brush dry-loaded in a darker ink tone. Hold the brush upright and paint the joint while the stem is still damp.

Canes and joints. Paint each section in one stroke. The edge of the cane should be distinct. Add the knots at the joints with darker ink tone (a and b show two different methods of painting the knots)

Branch

The branches shoot out from the joints alternately. They also grow section by section. A branch begins to grow from one side of a knotted joint, and grows upwards from the joint. The next branch begins at the next alternate knotted joint, but on the opposite side of the stem.

Use a no. 5 brush, dry-loaded in medium-dark ink. With the tip of the upright brush draw the branch section by section. Apply a little pressure at the beginning and at the end of each section. Conceal the brush tip while making the stroke so that the branches will not appear pointed at the end. The bigger main branches also have joints, but there is no need to leave spaces for them. Simply make a short stop at the joint and continue your brush movement.

Leaves

The leaves grow in clusters from the side branches and smaller branches. On the main bamboo stem leaves grow only from the topmost section. They do not sprout from the rest of the main stem.

The bamboo leaf is broad and flat tapering to a point. The closer the leaves are to the stem, the smaller their size. The leaves at the tips of the branches are larger.

Moist-load a no. 2 brush in dark ink. Hold the brush upright, pointing the tip towards the branch. Press down at the

Bamboo leaves. A cluster may contain two, three, four or five leaves. Some are arranged horizontally, some vertically

base and paint the leaf in one steady quick stroke. Drag the bristles a little at the middle for a broader effect, and release them towards the tip for a pointed effect. The result is that the base is round and full whilst the tip is sharp and pointed. Leaves in the foreground should appear moist and rich and should therefore be painted in darker tones. Paint leaves in the background in lighter tones. Re-load the brush as often as is necessary.

A cluster of leaves should give a sense of movement and suppleness. This can be achieved through the arrangements of the leaf-patterns. Vary the sizes — big, small, broad, slender, long and short. Vary the spacing too, placing some leaves closer together, and others further apart. You can also criss-cross the leaves in interesting patterns or paint them in layers.

CONTOUR STYLE IN INK AND COLOUR

To paint the bamboo contour style, start with the main stem, then paint the branches, and lastly the leaf clusters.

Branch and stem

Using a no. 5 brush, dry-loaded in a dark ink tone, outline the stem and the branches. After the outlines are dry, apply light green evenly by using a no. 3 brush, moist-loaded. (Mix indigo and yellow to obtain light green.) Apply a second layer of mineral green mixed with a little umber while the paper is still slightly damp.

Leaves

Method I Use a no. 3 brush, moist-loaded with two or three colour tones (black, indigo and yellow). Place the tip of your brush at the base of the leaf, and make one brushstroke to form one half of the leaf. Form the other half of the leaf along the vein but leave a narrow white line to serve as the vein.

Method II Using a no. 2 brush, moist-loaded, apply indigo shade evenly to form the leaves. After they are dry, apply a layer of light green.

Method III Use a no. 2 brush, moist-loaded in two or three tones of green. Starting from the base, form the leaf in one quick, upright brushstroke. After the leaf is dry, draw the leaf veins in white starting from the base to the tip.

OPPOSITE *Bamboo in the rain. The branches appear heavy, weighed down by rain. The shorter and thicker branches are sturdier, and bend only slightly. The thinner and longer the branches, the more pronounced the bend. The bamboo leaves point downwards. Some twist near the base of the leaf, some at the tip*

BELOW *Bamboo in the wind. The branches and leaves move with the wind. The tips of the leaves curl upwards in its intensity. Although bending in wind, the bigger branches appear strong and firm. The stem is painted first. The clusters of leaves point to the right*

BOTTOM LEFT *Bamboo in the snow. After painting the stem, branches and leaves, dot those surfaces, the branches and the leaf clusters in a pale ink tone, or white, to indicate snow flakes or accumulations of snow. Bear in mind the direction of the wind when dotting the snow*

BELOW *Hanging bamboo. Bamboo growing from the crevices of a cliff appears to hang downwards, and creates an impression of leaves swaying in the breeze. The tips of the hanging bamboo leaves turn slightly upwards, but do not appear weak*

CHRYSANTHEMUM

The chrysanthemum is the fourth of the noble plants. It blooms in the ninth month of the Chinese Lunar Calendar, during autumn when all the flowers have already begun to wither. There are countless species of chrysanthemum and they come in a multitude of colours. A chrysanthemum blossom has many petals, radiating out in circles from the centre. Some species have only one layer of petals, whilst others have several. The flowers range in size from very small blooms, about 25 mm (1 in) in diameter, to blooms that are the size of an open palm. The flower head also varies in shape, and may be circular, dome-shaped or disc-shaped. The petals come in all shapes and sizes; long and broad; short and broad; short and rounded; short and pointed; and long, curled and narrow.

First paint the chrysanthemum flower, then the calyx, stem and stalk, and lastly the leaves. When painting a chrysanthemum blossom with petals in multiple layers, you should keep in mind the following:

- the size of the petal varies according to its position in the flower head; whether it is in front or behind the other petals, or whether it is presenting a side view or a full view
- the arrangement of the petals in a particular bloom depends on the position of that bloom in the whole composition
- the petals of half-opened flowers hold tightly together
- the petals become progressively larger the further away they are from the centre

CONTEMPORARY STYLE

Flower

Use a no. 2 or 3 brush moist-loaded in two or three tones. Start with the petals in the innermost layer of the flower head, and paint progressively outward. Apply a single upright brushstroke for each petal. The pressure and tone may vary from petal to petal.

For a blossom that is fully opened, form a circle at the centre of the flower with dots applied in dark tone. Wash the

A spray of chrysanthemum in contemporary style

centre of the flower with light ink tone and then apply white dots over it. For colour compositions, use vermilion mixed with yellow and white; or crimson red mixed with indigo and white; mineral blue mixed with pink and white; or crimson red mixed with pink and white.

Calyx

Use a no. 3 brush, moist-loaded in light tone. With the tip of the an upright brush pointing towards the base of the flower head, apply pressure and move the brush towards the base. Apply three to seven brushstrokes to form a calyx. For colour compositions, use light green.

Stalks

Use a no. 4 brush moist-loaded in medium tone. Hold the brush in an upright position and apply a slender brushstroke downwards from the base of each flower. As you move along, leave spaces in between the stalks for the long stem and large leaves. For colour compositions, use light green mixed with umber.

Stem

Use a no. 3 brush dry-loaded in dark tone. Starting from the bottom of the painting, apply one slender upright push brushstroke up towards the base of the flower. Gradually decrease pressure as you move along, to reduce the thickness of the stem. For long stems, you may stop for a moment to gather strength for the second half of your push brushstroke. For colour compositions, use green mixed with umber.

Leaves

The chrysanthemum leaf can be painted using the two-brushstroke technique. (See chapter 4 for illustrations.) When painting the leaves, keep in mind the following:

- light tone is used for new leaves and the underside of leaves
- dark tone is used for big leaves and old leaves
- a darker tone is used for withered leaves
- apply shading over each leaf to give form and texture

Use a no. 2 brush wet-loaded. Hold the brush in either an oblique or an upright position to form half of the leaf. Make another stroke to form the other half. Add the vein along the thread of space in the centre

which the two brushstrokes have formed. Using a no. 5 brush dry-loaded in dark tone add in the veins with the tip of an upright brush.

For young and healthy leaves, add in the veins before the leaves are completely dry. For old and withered leaves, add the veins after the leaves are dry. For colour compositions, use light green for new leaves; green for matured leaves; and dark green and umber for withered leaves.

A spray of chrysanthemum in contour style

CONTOUR STYLE

For ink compositions, using a no. 5 brush, dry-loaded in lighter tone, outline the flowers and calyx, then the stalks and stem, and lastly the leaves. After the first outline is dry, apply another fine line over it in medium ink tone. For colour compositions, and in this instance for a yellow chyrsanthemum, the method is as follows.

Flower and calyx

Use a no. 5 brush, dry-loaded in light tone, to outline the petals and calyx.

For petals which show the underside, apply an even layer of white mixed with yellow, using a no. 2 brush, moist-loaded. Apply

umber to the tip and wash it
down to the base of the petal
with a clean wet brush. Dip the
tip of a no. 5 brush in white, and
draw fine parallel lines to form
the veins.

For petals which show the top-
side, apply an even layer of
white. Then apply indigo to the
tip and wash it down. Use umber
for the fine veins.

Stalks and stem

After outlining the stalks and
stem in light tone, apply light
green evenly over them, with a
no. 3 brush moist-loaded. After
the first wash is dry, apply a
layer of mineral green. Shade the
stem using light umber.

Leaves and veins

Outline the leaves in light tone.
The veins can be outlined in
medium tone. The veins can also
be outlined by drawing two fine
parallel lines leaving a thin
thread of space in between. Use a
no. 3 brush, wet-loaded, for the
underside of the leaves, first
applying a layer of light green.
While the leaf is damp, apply
mineral green along the centre of
the leaf and wash with a clean
wet brush to the edge.

For the top-side of the leaves
and veins, apply a wash of pale
indigo blue. You may leave the
veins white if you wish. Apply
washes of different shades of
yellow-green or dark-green to
the leaf sections, depending on
their positions.

Basket of chrysanthemums

BIBLIOGRAPHY

BACHHOFER L., *A short history of Chinese Art*, B.T. Batsford Ltd, London 1947

FONG WEN, *Sung and Yuan Painting*, The Metropolitan Museum of Art, New York 1973

FU SHEN C.Y., *Studies in Chinese Calligraphy – Traces of The Brush*, Yale University Press 1980

GOODALL J.A., *Heaven and Earth*, Shambhala Publication Inc, Boulder, Colorado 1979

HUTT J., *Understanding Far Eastern Art*, Phaidon Press Ltd, Oxford 1987

SILCOCK A., *Introduction to Chinese Art*, Oxford University Press, London 1935

STREHLNEEK E.A., *Chinese Pictorial Art*, The Commercial Press Ltd, Shanghai 1914

SULLIVAN M., *Chinese Art in the Twentieth Century*, Faber & Faber, London 1959

SULLIVAN M., *A Short History of Chinese Art*, Faber & Faber, London 1967

SULLIVAN M., *The Arts of China*, University of California Press, Berkeley 1976

Cypress trees

SUPPLIERS

There are a few specialist Chinese art material suppliers in Britain, but ink, paper, brushes and other equipment are available or can be ordered from most reputable art dealers.

Useful addresses in case of difficulty are:

Guanghwa Co
7–9 Newport Place
London WC2H 7JR

Neal Street East
3–5 Neal Street
Covent Garden
London WC2H 9PU

Collet's Chinese Bookshop
40 Great Russell Street
London WC1B 3PJ

Chinese Arts Centre
50 High Street
Oxford OX1 4AS

Kam Cheung
28–30 Burleigh Street
Cambridge CB1 1DG

Centre of Restoration & Arts
8 Adelaide Street
St Albans
Herts AL3 5NP

Greyfriars Art Shop
1 Greyfriars Place
Edinburgh EH1 2QQ

In addition, Green & Stone of Chelsea, 259 King's Road, London NW3, stock antique Chinese paper and occasionally antique Chinese ink stones

Of course, the best place to send for materials is the Far East itself, though obviously the process is longer. Try:

Tsing's Book & Art
Blk 231, Bain Street 03–17
Bras Basah Complex
Singapore 0718

The following are useful addresses in the USA:

Chinese Culture Co
736–738 7th Street, NW
Washington DC 20001

Oriental Culture Enterprises
22 Pell Street
New York
NY 10013

Chinese Culture Co
126 N 10th Street
Philadelphia
PA 19107

Chinese Culture Co
843 Clement Street
San Francisco
CA 94118

INDEX

INDEX